WANDSWORTH
PAST

First published 1998
by Historical Publications Ltd
32 Ellington Street, London N7 8PL
(Tel: 0171-607 1628)

ISBN 0 948667 47 8
British Library Cataloguing-in-Publication Data
A catalogue record for this book is available from the British Library

Typeset in Palatino by Historical Publications Ltd
Reproduction by G & J Graphics, London EC2
Printed by Edelvives, Zaragoza, Spain

WANDSWORTH PAST

Dorian Gerhold

HISTORICAL PUBLICATIONS

Acknowledgements

This book could not have been written without considerable assistance from numerous people, but especially from Rita Ensing, who provided much of the material for the early history and some other aspects, and from Tony Evans, who gave me the benefit of his extensive researches on eighteenth-century Wandsworth. I am also most grateful for the help received from Pat Astley-Cooper, Keith Bailey, Sue Barber, Michael Bull, Meredith Davis, Peter Edwards, Peter Gerhold, Pamela Greenwood, Janet Koss, Patrick Loobey, Stewart McLaughlin, Richard Milward, Helen Osborn and Tony Shaw.

The Illustrations

The following have kindly given permission for illustrations to be used:
British Library 10 (*Althorp Papers, P13, part 1*), 42 (*The Miller, 1 June 1885*), 50 (*Althorp Papers P2*), 96 (*Add 36489A, No. 103*)
Michael Bull: 92
Private Collection (photograph: Courtauld Institute of Art): 34
Derbyshire Record Office: 56
Fazl Mosque: 130
Dorian Gerhold: 2,4, 6, 21, 23, 24, 26, 30, 31, 51, 60, 65, 71, 72, 78, 100, 110, 113, 156, 158, 162, 164, 165, 170
Peter Gerhold: 12, 27, 29, 52, 61, 79, 83, 134, 143, 151, 168
Glaxo Wellcome Heritage Archives: 185
Guildhall Library, London: 36
Historical Publications: 32, 93, 94, 153, 155
London Borough of Lambeth Archives: 121, 167,
London Metropolitan Archives: 87, 136, 139
Patrick Loobey: 7, 80, 82, 85, 90, 91, 98, 99, 101, 103, 104, 105, 108, 112, 115, 137, 138, 140, 172, 173, 175, 176, 179, 180, 182, 183, 186
Merton Libraries and Heritage Services: 142
Museum of London: 20, 28, 63, 135, 157
National Portrait Gallery: 53
Northamptonshire Record Office: 33 (*SOX 101*), 54 (*SOX 342*)
Royal Hospital for Neuro-Disability: 149
Surrey Record Office: 9, 16, 18,
Wandsworth Borough Council: 5
Wandsworth Challenge Partnership: 198
Wandsworth Historical Society: 11, 68
Wandsworth Local History Collection: 1, 3, 8, 15, 17, 25, 37, 38, 39, 40, 43, 44, 48, 59, 62, 64, 67, 70, 75, 76, 81, 86, 88, 89, 95, 97, 106, 107, 109, 111, 114, 116, 117, 119, 123, 124, 125, 126, 127, 128, 129, 132, 141, 144, 145, 146, 147, 148, 150, 152, 154, 159, 160, 161, 163, 166, 171, 177, 178, 181, 184, 187, 188, 189, 190, 191, 192, 195, 196, 197
Wandsworth Museum: 14, 19, 22, 41, 47, 49, 55, 57, 58, 66, 73, 74, 84, 102, 118, 120, 122, 131, 133, 169, 193, 194
Wimbledon Museum: 69, 77
Yale Center for British Art: 13, 35
Young's Brewery: 45, 46, 174

Contents

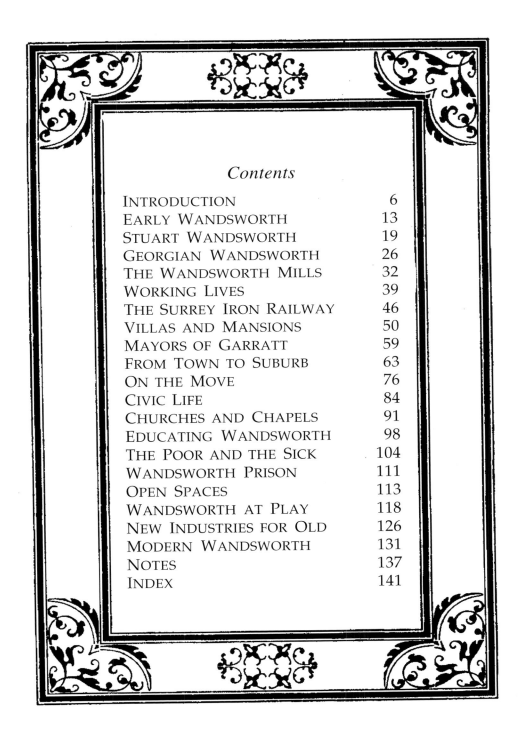

1. *'View of Wandsworth from Mr Van Necks', published c.1750. Wandsworth is seen from the west across North Field, where the small gunpowder house is visible near the river at the far end of the field. Just beyond it is a large building at Point Pleasant, which had probably been Edward Barker's warehouse for iron, and to its right an irregular group of buildings which must have been those used for the manufacture of frying pans. The windmill in the distance is a little beyond where Wandsworth Bridge is now; the one on the right formed part of the Middle Mill.*

Introduction

Wandsworth's history is unique in south-west London, and the reason for this was the River Wandle. Its rapid fall (124 feet in just nine miles) made it a fast-flowing river, one of the most powerful rivers for driving mills in the country. Such a source of power so close to London was inevitably used intensively, initially for flour milling and later for other industries. Few other parishes in the country in about 1800 had such a range of industries as Wandsworth.

Industries required workers, and thus encouraged the construction of workers' tenements. Industrial potential also attracted foreigners, sometimes bringing new processes with them. On the other hand, industry and a large working class repelled the well-to-do, whose villas were so important in neighbouring Clapham and Putney parishes. Lack of appeal to the wealthy meant in turn that there was relatively cheap property for schools and charitable institutions. The Wandle also shaped the pattern of development within the parish: its north-south valley contained most of the industry, while Wandsworth's relatively few villas were built on the higher ground of East Hill and West Hill. This correlation of height and affluence (and of lowness and poverty) was largely maintained when Wandsworth eventually became a suburb.

The Thames was also important to Wandsworth, providing cheap transport to London and much work for watermen and fishermen, but did not dominate its history in the way that it did at neighbouring Putney. Unlike at Putney and Battersea, the village at Wandsworth was well inland from the Thames, behind the marshy area at the Wandle's mouth. Instead, Wandsworth's most important feature after the Wandle was the major road from east to west through Wandsworth High Street, linking London and the south-west. By 1569 there was a stone bridge, probably of medieval origin, where this road crosses the Wandle,[1] and it was naturally around this point that the village of Wandsworth had developed. The road's present-day importance needs no emphasis. Until the nineteenth century there were no crossings of the Wandle south of the High Street, except for pedestrians, until beyond Summerstown. The southern part of the parish, away from major routes, remained relatively remote, and was developed for suburban housing much later than the northern part.

Another important aspect of Wandsworth's position was its closeness to London, which pro-

2. *Cottages on Frogs Island of about 1830, but apparently including at the far end earlier buildings once part of Henry Gardiner's calico-printing works. They were demolished in 1932, and their site is now the northern part of the Arndale Centre's Traders Hall.*

vided a voracious market for Wandsworth's agricultural and industrial produce. As early as 1086, the manors in the north-east of Surrey, which included Wandsworth, had the highest recorded population and highest number of plough-teams per square mile in the county.[2]

Although industry made Wandsworth distinctive, the parish also had a large agricultural population, reflecting its large size. The ancient parish of Wandsworth, which is the subject of this book, included the present Earlsfield and Southfields, and did not entirely correspond to what is now thought of as Wandsworth, particularly towards the west, where it extended to East Putney Station and a large part of Wimbledon Common (as far as a point still marked by a large stone near the windmill). Despite the large area, there were no subsidiary settlements until the nineteenth century apart from the hamlet of Garratt, around what is now the Leather Bottle pub.

THE WANDLE

Given its importance to Wandsworth's story, the Wandle requires some further introduction, especially as it has been so greatly altered by the reduction in its flow, by culverting and by pollution. Its water originates in the North Downs, passing underground through the chalk and emerging at a line of springs on the north side of the Downs from Croydon to Carshalton, at which places the two branches of the river began. This distant origin, and the lack of any significant tributaries except the Graveney, meant that its flow was unusually even, not declining substantially in summer and rarely causing flooding.[3] The latter changed in the nineteenth century as suburban development increased the speed with which water ran off the neighbouring land. In the seventeenth century it was recorded that the Wandle never froze – a consequence of its rapid flow.[4]

Another important characteristic of the Wandle was its cleanness. Aubrey's much-quoted remark, in the late seventeenth century, about 'the sink of the country', so often misquoted as a reference to the river at Wandsworth, actually referred to the

3. *The Wandle bridge in about 1900. The bridge was rebuilt in 1820 and 1912. To its left the Wandle today runs underneath the Arndale Centre. In the background are the Bull public house (rebuilt in the 1880s and destroyed in 1940) and the tower of All Saints Church (as altered in 1841).*

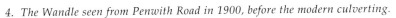

4. *The Wandle seen from Penwith Road in 1900, before the modern culverting.*

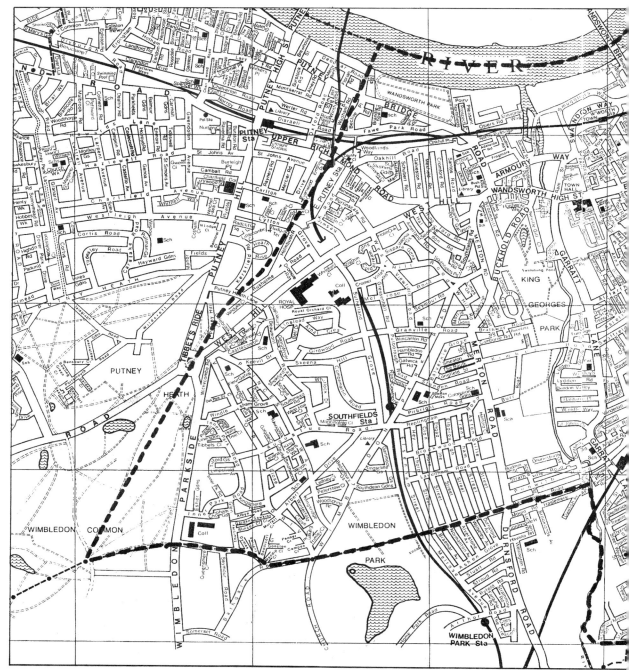

5. *Street map of modern Wandsworth, with the ancient parish boundary marked as a thick broken line. For clarity, modern street names have been used in the text of this book. The most important changes are that Love Lane is now the Wandsworth part of Putney Bridge Road, Slough Lane (later North Street) is now Fairfield Street and South Street is now the northern part of Garratt Lane.*

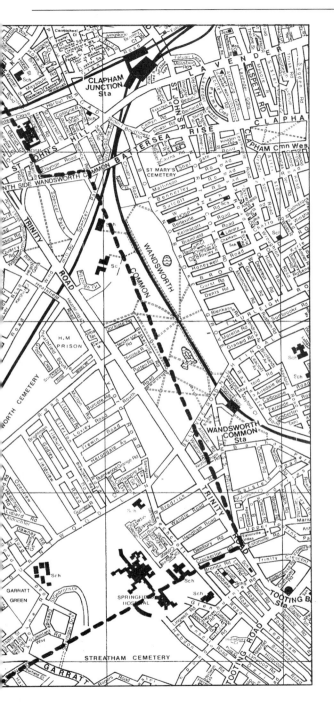

bridge,[5] and probably related to the cost to the county (or 'country' in seventeenth-century parlance) of maintaining a substantial bridge over a fast-flowing stream – hence a sink into which the county threw its money. If the Wandle had been a dirty river, it could not possibly have sustained the dyeing, bleaching and calico-printing which flourished on its banks, all of which needed clean water. Nor could it have been noted, as it was, for its trout. Many of the works dumped waste in the river, but the strong flow apparently diluted it without difficulty. The Wandle remained a trout river until the nineteenth century; in 1852 the disappearance of trout from the lower reaches was attributed to a fire earlier in the century at an oil mill (presumably the Garratt oil mill), which had killed the trout downstream, after which they had been unable to make their way back up the river past the mill weirs.[6] Increasing population, especially at Croydon, was probably the main reason for the river's deteriorating state in the nineteenth century, as abstraction of water reduced its flow and the quantity of sewage increased.

The Wandle's course was altered centuries before the first maps, as its main channel became essentially a succession of level pools between the mills. It occupied much more of central Wandsworth than the present channel. North of the village, until the eighteenth century, it swung west to reach the Thames some way from the present outlet, and there were several lesser channels, highly useful for shipping, together with much marshy ground used to grow osiers (willow shoots employed in thatching and basket-making). South of the village there was a sidewater, perhaps an earlier course, extending almost as far west as Broomhill Road and rejoining the main course under the present Arndale Centre. The sidewater was straightened (as the New Cut) in the nineteenth century, and was filled in in 1967-8.[7]

The Wandle brought work and (for some) prosperity, but it also made Wandsworth a dangerous place. In 1254-5, for example, Matilda, daughter of Ranulph, was crushed by the wheel of a watermill at Wandsworth. In 1789 a daughter of Mr Blackmore, bolting-cloth manufacturer, slipped off a step at the bottom of the family's garden into the river, was carried into the Middle Mill and drowned; and in 1809, the daughter of a mealman was leaning on a rail at the mill-head at the Upper Mill when it gave way, and she was soon entangled in one of the mill wheels and killed.[8]

6. *Looking down West Hill towards the High Street in about 1900. The George and Dragon pub (closed in 1903) is on the left.*

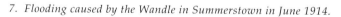

7. *Flooding caused by the Wandle in Summerstown in June 1914.*

Early Wandsworth

The bed of clay on which greater London lies is overlain in the Wandle valley by alluvium, creating valuable meadows, and along both the Wandle and the Thames by gravel and sand river terraces suitable for cultivation. Numerous hand axes and flint flakes found in the Earlsfield and St Ann's Hill areas and in the Thames suggest occupation in the Early Palaeolithic period (500,000 to 35,000 years ago).[1] Of later periods, the Neolithic Period (4500-2200 BC), when people first began farming and living a more settled life, has provided some flint implements and pottery, found on East Hill and along the Thames, the Bronze Age (2200-800 BC) has yielded a founder's hoard and lumps of metal from the gas works site by the Thames, part of a gold ring from Point Pleasant and other items, and the Iron Age (800 BC-50 AD) has provided metalwork and pottery.[2] Finds of metalwork and pottery from the late Bronze Age and subsequent periods on the Thames foreshore by Wandsworth Park may indicate a settlement now being eroded there. Also, an Iron Age sword and sheath (4th-3rd century BC) and Iron Age shield bosses have been found on the Thames foreshore, though they do not necessarily indicate settlement at Wandsworth.

It is reckoned that by the late Iron Age (50 BC-50 AD) and in the Roman period (c.50-410AD)

8. One of the Iron Age shield bosses found in the Thames at Wandsworth near the mouth of the Wandle.

settlement in the London area was probably as dense as in the early medieval period, and there is evidence of activity beside the Thames at Wandsworth throughout the Roman period. Finds include a late Roman coin hoard from the Thames-side, now in Wandsworth Museum, and a cremation burial of the second century AD at the junction of St Ann's Crescent and Allfarthing Lane.[3] There is both archaeological and documentary evidence for an east-west Roman road through Mortlake and Putney, roughly on the line of the Upper Richmond Road,[4] and this may well have continued through Wandsworth towards Stane Street.

In Anglo-Saxon times there was a single large estate covering Battersea and Wandsworth. It was granted in 693 to the nuns of Barking Abbey, but after the Abbey was sacked by the Danes the estate reverted to the Crown. In 1067 William the Conqueror granted it to Westminster Abbey 'for their provision of victuals' in exchange for Windsor Forest, and it remained in the Abbey's possession until 1540. William's grant included the 'berewick' of Wandsworth, 'berewick' usually meaning an outlying part of an estate.[5] Thus, even by 1067, though forming part of a larger manor, Wandsworth was a distinct place, evidently with its own boundaries, and such subdivisions within estates were often of great antiquity.

The first references to Wandsworth are as Wendles Wurthe in a later copy of a charter of 693, and in 1067 as Wendleswurthe. The name is usually taken to mean Wendel's farm or settlement. The name 'Wandle' appears to have derived from Wandsworth rather than vice versa. The 693 charter calls the river 'hlida burnan', and 'hlida' is probably the Old English 'hlyde' or 'loud one', alluding to the river as a fast-flowing and therefore noisy one. The monks of Westminster Abbey called it the Lutbourne, a variant of the same name, as late as 1469. Locally it was often referred to simply as 'the river'. The earliest reference to its present name (in the Latinised form 'Vandalis') is from 1586.[6]

In 1086, most of Wandsworth, being part of the Battersea estate, was included in Domesday Book's entry for Battersea, but two aspects of that entry are specific to Wandsworth, or largely so. There were seven mills, worth £42. 9s. 8d. Undoubtedly all or most of these were on the Wandle, since it was a fast-flowing river later famous for its mills, unlike the only other candidate, Battersea's Falcon Brook. If the value was correctly recorded, the mills accounted for an extraordinary 56% of the manor's total value. There was also £6 'from the tolls of Wandsworth'. The most likely explanation for these is some form of landing fee for boats, and the mills certainly needed boats conveying grain and flour. By 1086 there were also two much smaller manors in Wandsworth, one held by William, son of Ansculf, Sheriff of Surrey, and the other by the French monastery of St Wandrille.[7]

MANORS

The manorial structure in Wandsworth later became much more complicated, apparently mainly because in the twelfth century some of the Abbey's tenants succeeded in converting life tenancies into fixed-rent tenancies which could be inherited and became separate manors. By the end of the fourteenth century, after the monks had repurchased all but one of the separate holdings, there were four manors, each with their own home farm and each with a share in a single open field system where their lands were intermingled.

The manor house of Battersea and Wandsworth Manor was in Battersea, and the Wandsworth berewick was administered from the Savage Farm, which stood just north of Wandsworth's church. In 1225, when Westminster Abbey's sources of income were formally divided between the Abbot and the Prior and Convent (i.e. the monks), Battersea and Wandsworth was one of the manors allocated to the monks, together with the two parish churches. (Wandsworth had its own church by 1157.)

Allfarthing Manor was an agglomeration of three estates or fees which had probably once been part of the manor of Battersea and Wandsworth. These were Allfarthing (meaning half of a quarter of a fee), Barking fee and Finches fee. The Abbey had repurchased them all by 1378, and from 1403 they were treated as one manor. It was largely in the east of the parish, but included meadows by the Wandle, strips in the open fields and a small meadow in Battersea Marsh.[8]

Downe, the smallest manor, may have been part of the manor held by William Fitz-Ansculf in 1086, since in the thirteenth century it was described as 'a fief of the honour of Dudley', of which Fitz-Ansculf's successors were lords. The Abbot purchased it from Robert de Fynnesford (also known as Robert de Doune) and his wife Alice in 1370. Its lands were predominantly in the south-west of the parish, but were intermingled with those of Dunsford Manor rather than forming a solid block. The south-west part of the village and strips in the open fields also belonged to it. Its manor house was to the south of the High Street, between the present Buckhold Road and Hardwick's Way.

Dunsford Manor was held from the thirteenth century by Merton Priory. Its lands, like Downe's,

9. *Allfarthing Manor House in 1633. North is to the left, and the east-west road is Allfarthing Lane, with the kink between the present St Ann's Crescent and St Ann's Park Road. The manor house was apparently the buildings to the west; those to the east (the site of the later Elm Lodge) are marked as a sheepcote (a shelter for sheep).*

were largely in the south-west of the parish and included strips in the open fields. Its manor house was in Merton Road on the present Territorial Army site. South of Burntwood Lane, but also with some land by the Wandle, was an estate called the Garratt, which was apparently not part of the manorial system but was usually held with Dunsford Manor. The name is thought to refer to a watch house or watch tower.

The manor houses only needed to provide somewhere for manorial courts to be held and for the Monk Bailiff (in Westminster's case) to stay when inspecting the estate, and each comprised a hall with a chamber attached, together with stables, barns, granaries and other outbuildings. Wandsworth became a favourite place with the monks for convalescence.[9]

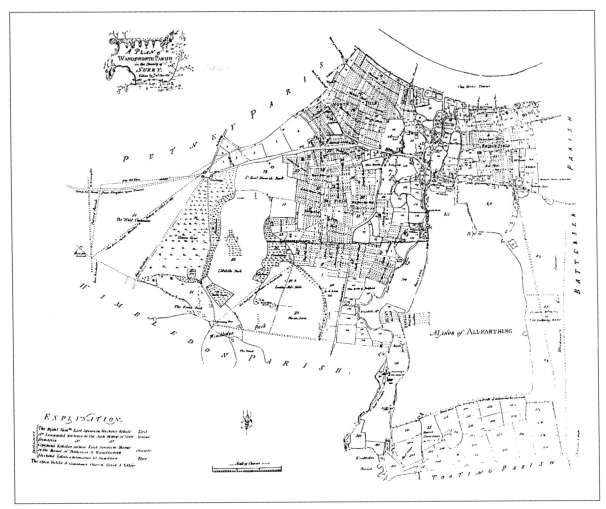

10. *John Corris's map of Wandsworth, drawn for Earl Spencer in 1787. Despite later changes, it shows many of the features of medieval Wandsworth, including the three main open fields (Bridge, North and South Fields) and the smaller open field called Austins Croft (south of the Upper Richmond Road). The most important post-medieval change was the extension of Wimbledon Park into the south-west part of the parish, replacing the closes of Downe and Dunsford Manors and part of the West Common. South Field had once been more extensive, and the West Common had included the area by Park Side marked 'Game Cover' and some land to its east, together with the closes shown north of West Hill (extending to the present Keswick Road). Earl Spencer did not yet own Allfarthing Manor in 1787, so little detail is given for it.*

FIELDS AND FARMING

At some time between the eleventh century and 1247, when South Field and North Field are first mentioned, Wandsworth acquired a system of open fields, and perhaps at the same time settlement became concentrated in the area of the later village. Each open field was divided into shots, or groups of strips, which were the unit of cultivation, but after the crops had been harvested each field formed a single grazing area. As late as 1787,

Corris's map shows Putney Bridge Road west of Point Pleasant as an unfenced track, across which cattle grazing in North Field could wander at will; indeed the strips of Thames Shot crossed the road, which had probably once been regularly ploughed up. Administering an open field system shared by four manors must have been difficult: in the sixteenth century Dunsford's manor court made regulations as if it was the only manor involved, but at least once, in 1581, the parish officials appointed a herdsman to control the pasturing of cows.[10] Much of the southern part of the parish was enclosed by the sixteenth century, if not much earlier.

Wandsworth's largest area of common land was the West Common (or Heath), part of what is now Wimbledon Common or Putney Heath. It extended much further east than it does now – in places east of the present Princes Way. The East Common, shared with Battersea, now forms Wandsworth Common, but it too has been much reduced in area. Towards the south were two small commons, Garratt Great Green, which survives, and Garratt Little Green, at the junction of Garratt Lane and Summerstown, now lost. The latter was probably the small common known until the seventeenth century as Heyford Green. North of what is now Frogmore was Hogmore Green, which provided access to an arm of the Wandle where goods could be shipped. The commons tended to be the parish's least fertile areas, unsuitable for growing crops. The smaller manors shared in the commons, and apparently had their own defined areas, such as that known as Allfarthing Piece on the East Common.[11]

Westminster Abbey's records provide much information about life in Wandsworth from the late fourteenth century. The manors were in the day-to-day charge of a paid servant called a sergeant (a reeve in the case of Battersea and Wandsworth), who was left little scope for initiative by the Monk Bailiff at Westminster. Each manor had a carter, a ploughman and a shepherd. There were large flocks of sheep: Allfarthing kept about 300 wethers, which produced superior fleeces, while Downe had about 200 ewes with their lambs and three or more rams. The main crop was oats, but wheat, rye and barley were also grown, together with peas, beans and vetch (used for a kind of soup called potage and as fodder). The manors' corn was sent by boat to the Monk Granger at Westminster. Allfarthing Manor had a tile kiln, constructed in 1365, which was probably the one discovered recently at the junction of Wandsworth High Street and St Ann's Hill. By the end of the fourteenth century the tenants' burden of work on the lands kept in hand by the Abbey had largely been converted to money payments.[12]

CITIZENS AND COURTIERS

London citizens and courtiers had begun to build up estates in Wandsworth by the early fifteenth century. One such was Nicholas Mauduit, whose memorial brass (much mutilated) survives in All Saints Church. He held the important office of Serjeant at Arms under Henry IV and Henry V, and in 1414 he became Serjeant at Arms to the

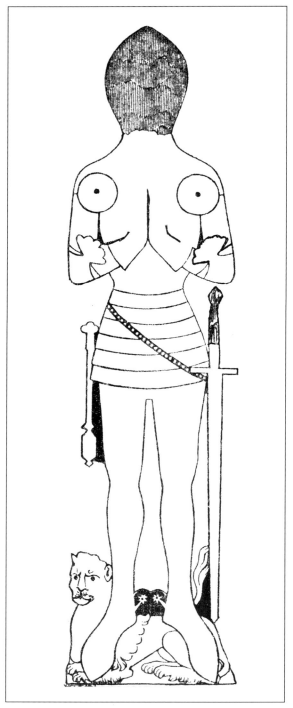

11. *The brass commemorating Nicholas Mauduit (d.1420).*

12. (Above) The Sword House, at the foot of West Hill
(where the police station is now), probably dating from
the sixteenth century and demolished in about 1875. It
was said to have been occupied by an army officer who
had brought home from the Battle of Culloden in 1745 a
quantity of Highland swords, which he arranged as a
decorative feature on the wall outside the house, giving
its name to the house.

13. (Right) The back of The Gables, on North Side,
probably of the late sixteenth or early seventeenth
century, drawn by Francis Grose, who occupied the
house in the 1760s and 1770s. It was demolished in
1907, and 72-80 North Side now occupy the site.

14. A house on the south side of the High Street between St Ann's Hill and Garratt Lane.

15. The Parsonage, on the south side of the High Street where South Thames College is now, drawn by R.B. Schnebbelie in 1810.

House of Commons. He started buying land in Allfarthing and Downe in 1406, and the fact that, after his death in 1420, his brass was placed at Wandsworth almost certainly means that he had used some of his holdings there as a country retreat.[13]

Another important landholder, though his house was in Battersea, was Laurence Booth, Archbishop of York. He started purchasing land in 1460 (when Bishop of Durham), his Wandsworth acquisitions being largely in the east of the parish. On his death he left the estate to the See of York as a country retreat from their London house in Whitehall. Later, when the manors were in the hands of the Crown, they attracted minor courtiers such as Thomas Hayward, yeoman of the Guard under Henry VIII, Edward VI, Mary I and Elizabeth I, and John Powell, Yeoman of the Bottles under Queen Elizabeth and Clerk of the King's Cellar under James I. Five inhabitants were excused paying tax in 1594 because they were in the Queen's service.[14]

THE REFORMATION

At the dissolution of the monasteries, the estates of Westminster Abbey and Merton Priory passed to the Crown (in 1540 and 1538 respectively). The Crown sometimes leased them out and eventually granted them all away. The manors experienced many changes of ownership, the families with the longest tenure, prior to the Spencers, being the Smiths at Dunsford from 1569 to 1664, the St Johns at Battersea and Wandsworth from 1627 (though

earlier through marriage) to 1763, the Porters at Allfarthing from 1628 to 1811, the Brodricks at Dunsford from 1664 to the present and Elizabeth Howland and her heirs, the Dukes of Bedford, at Downe from 1698 to 1792.

The churchwardens' accounts, commencing in 1545, record the changes in the parish church, such as the obtaining of new service books in English and a communion table and the removal of the stone altar, the rood loft and thirteen wooden or alabaster images. Another casualty was the hermitage, which seems to have stood at the junction of West Hill and the Upper Richmond Road, where the hermit could be of service to travellers. In 1524 fourpence was paid to 'the ermyt at Wandsworth' on behalf of Thomas Manners, 13th Baron Ros, who was travelling through Surrey.[15]

Some people resisted the changes. John Griffiths, Vicar of Wandsworth was hung, drawn and quartered in 1539, apparently for denying the royal supremacy over the Church.[16] Later, others wanted more radical change, and in 1572 the first Presbyterian meeting in England was established at Wandsworth. Its members were extreme puritans, opposed to church government by bishops and archbishops and to the Book of Common Prayer. However, it was clearly not an assembly of local people: those listed as leading members included Nicholas Crane of Roehampton, 'Smith of Micham' and two London Ministers.[17] Thomas Smith of Mitcham held property at Wandsworth, including Dunsford Manor, which was probably the reason for the meeting being at Wandsworth.

Stuart Wandsworth

THE VILLAGE

The map of Allfarthing Manor surveyed in 1633 provides our first glimpse of Wandsworth village. Jumbled together, largely in the High Street and the Plain, were the substantial houses of the minor gentry and merchants, the farmhouses and the smaller houses of the craftsmen and labourers. In modern terms, they extended in West Hill and the High Street from the Library to the junction with Fairfield Street, and from the Old Sergeant pub along Garratt Lane and the Plain; there were also a few in the Causeway, Frogmore, the part of Putney Bridge Road (then Love Lane) nearest Wandsworth High Street, East Hill, Fairfield Street and Waterside. The latter then occupied about 200 yards of the Thames bank west of the present Ship

pub. The map gives the impression of a straggly village, closely built-up only in the High Street and the Plain.

The hamlet of Garratt consisted of a few small houses on the west side of Garratt Lane. Dunsford Manor House is shown, as is a building just north of Garratt Green, and there was the farm of Garratt outside the map area, but otherwise the southern part of the parish was empty of dwellings.

The population was growing rapidly in the early seventeenth century – from about 1000 in the first decade to about 1800 in the 1640s, but growth then slowed: it was about 2100 at the end of the century, though this may reflect some under-recording of the Huguenots. The built-up area spread, notably to Point Pleasant and East Hill. Houses were increasingly of brick and tile, but in the 1660s at least some of the poor were living in thatched houses.[1]

One major restraint on population growth was

16. *The centre of Wandsworth on Gardiner's map, drawn in 1640 but based on a survey of 1633. North is to the left. Notable features include the Lower Mill, the navigable creek to Hogmore, the Middle Mill (then known as the Brazil Mill), Sir Thomas Brodrick's new house north of the church, the maypole at the corner of the Plain and the High Street, James Wilford's house south-west of the Wandle bridge, the Upper Mill (then known as the Middle Mill), Downe Manor House south of the High Street and the nearby parsonage barn.*

17. All Saints Church in 1750, prior to the rebuilding of 1779, showing the tower erected in 1630. In the background is the Middle Mill's windmill.

plague. 123 died in 1603-4, 52 in 1625, a few in most years from 1636 to 1648 and the astonishing total of 345 in 1665-6. The latter was about 19% of the entire population, much more than in neighbouring parishes such as Putney (about 7%) and almost the same as in London itself (about 18%).[2] The severity of the outbreak probably reflected overcrowding and insanitary conditions. Three pesthouses were erected, guarded by 'a watchhouse standing on wheeles'. Other parish expenses included 'locks staples and haspes to shutt up ye houses infected' and 'a wagon to draw ye corps to ye ground'. Later tradition was that the pits for burying victims were next to the parish's western boundary where East Putney Station is now and next to its eastern boundary where Garrick Close is now.[3]

The parish was administered by the Vestry, which had its own meeting place in the north-west corner of the church by 1657. In 1627 it was converted from an open vestry, which any ratepayer could attend, to a closed one, with fifteen members. By the 1660s it included many of the local industrialists, as well as one foreign immigrant, Abraham Hebert, merchant and dyer.[4] Later in the century the closed vestry disappeared, and by 1720 the minutes normally state that decisions were taken at a 'free and open Vestry'.

The parish played no direct part in the Civil Wars, but the wars affected it in several ways. An early casualty, even before war broke out, was the maypole, at the junction of the High Street and the Plain. This sort of entertainment was much disliked by puritans, and in 1640 the maypole was taken down. The Minister, Hugh Roberts, was nearly ejected in 1655, but the inhabitants signed a petition to Cromwell on his behalf stating that in his twelve years at Wandsworth his life had been exemplary and he had never committed misdemeanours such as preaching against the Government. Roberts survived.[5] The main impact of the Civil Wars may well have been the encouragement they gave to Wandsworth's metalworking industries, as discussed later.

EARNING A LIVING

The importance of the mills is indicated by the controversy over plans to pipe some of the Wandle water to London in 1610, which it was feared would deprive them of much of the water they needed. The four millers' households probably contained about 24 people. There were fourteen mealmen, whose households contained 63 people.

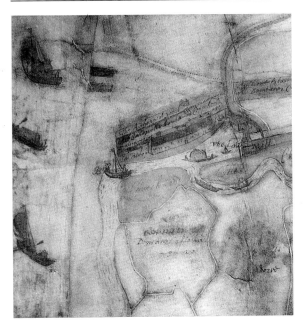

18. *A closer look at the Wandle near its mouth on Gardiner's map of 1633. It shows the Lower Mill astride the Wandle, the Causeway bridge to its right (required in the 1560s to be at least four feet wide), a long building (probably warehousing) and a variety of boats.*

Thirteen Wandsworth watermen claimed to have 'all their mayntenance and liveing by working in Wandsworth mill boates', and their households contained 61 people. They may have exaggerated their dependence on the mills, but on the other hand referred to 'a great number of millers, loaders, and wayghers, whom we leave unnamed'. Wandsworth also had 'many poore haglers whoe by the helpe & meanes of the said mill botes have their wares conveied to the Citie of London', which would otherwise have cost them more.[6]

Taking just the millers, mealmen and watermen working mill boats and their households, at least 148 people depended directly on the mills, or 13% of a population of about 1100. This probably excludes some who depended on the mills, such as those who conveyed wheat and flour between the mills and navigable water by packhorse. In 1663 complaint was made that 'keddars millers servants and other such like persons ... being many times drunck and disorderly ... drive great nombers of kedhorses loose through the streets and passages ... oftentimes in full speed', sometimes injuring or killing people.[7]

19. *Albert House, built in 1620, on the east side of Garratt Lane a little south of Malva Road. It ended its days as part of Voelker's gas mantle factory, and was demolished in about 1904. (Watercolour by A.E. Coleman, 1893.)*

20. One of the carved brackets from Albert House, now in the Museum of London.

At the start of the century, the other significant areas of employment were in agriculture and as watermen and fishermen. The main innovation in agriculture was the arrival of market gardening, and five gardeners are mentioned in the late 1620s.[8] Other than millers, brewers and an occasional weaver, no industrial occupations are recorded in wills and the parish registers until the 1630s. The growth of industry from the 1630s to the 1650s was by far the most important change in Wandsworth during the century, and is discussed in detail later. Frying pan manufacture began in the early 1630s, scarlet dyeing in the 1640s or 1650s, copper working by 1654, gunpowder milling in 1655 or 1656 and bleaching in 1657. More industries arrived with the Huguenots in the 1680s.

Between 1670 and 1686, a rough indication of the importance of different occupations can be obtained from the registers of baptisms and burials. Of the 325 individuals whose occupations are recorded then, about 20% were involved in agriculture (to whom the majority of the 16% described as labourer should probably be added), 14% were watermen or fishermen, 8% were millers or mealmen, 10% were in other industrial occupations (to whom should be added most of the 5% described as 'Dutchman' or 'Frenchman'), about 4% were supported by road transport (including innkeepers and wheelwrights) and 23% were involved in building or providing food, clothing or other services.

Although Wandsworth had many sources of work and was growing fast for much of the century, this did not make it prosperous. When the hearth (or chimney) tax was collected in 1664, 42%

of Wandworth's households were exempt on grounds of poverty, only a little more than in Battersea (36%), but far more than in Putney (23%) and Clapham (21%). 62% of Wandsworth's households lived in houses with only one or two hearths. Many families helped make ends meet by taking in London children to nurse.[9]

21. A house with Dutch gables, probably of the 1630s, in the High Street west of the church.

DUTCHMEN AND HUGUENOTS

The first of the many foreigners who settled in Wandsworth in the seventeenth century were the Dutch, although some of those described loosely as Dutch were probably French or Walloon (from an area now largely in Belgium). Most seem to have been migrants rather than refugees. The largest single contingent was the Dutchmen brought over to make frying pans in the early 1630s, and Dutchmen also seem to have been instrumental in establishing copper working and dyeing, and perhaps bleaching. They laid the foundations of industrial Wandsworth. However, there were also Dutchmen in more traditional occupations, such as John Blundell, waterman, in the 1680s. The name of Dutch Yard, south of the High Street, first mentioned in 1703, appears to record the residence there of John and Dorothy De Raedt in the late seventeenth century.[10]

Unlike the Dutchmen, the Huguenots (French Protestants) came as refugees. Frenchmen are occasionally recorded in Wandsworth prior to the 1680s, but large numbers arrived in that decade as a result of persecution by Louis XIV, culminating in 1685 in the revocation of the Edict of Nantes, which had granted them liberty. In 1682 a petition from 21 Wandsworth Huguenots explained that they had established some manufactures at Wandsworth and planned to establish others, that this had attracted some French Protestant workmen with their families and that others would settle there if they could have church services in their own language. This was necessary because most did not understand English and it was too expensive and time-consuming to go to the French Chapel at the Savoy.[11] A chapel was duly established.

The Huguenots' names tended to be anglicised, so it is difficult to estimate how many there were in Wandsworth, but the number was certainly substantial. There was a second influx, of Huguenots moving from London, in 1707-9.[12] They were welcome in new trades, but less so in established ones: in 1695 some dyers threatened to pull down the house of a French Protestant dyer at Wandsworth, and it was suggested that troops be deployed to keep the peace.[13] The Huguenots remained a strong element in eighteenth-century Wandsworth, but as one generation succeeded another they were gradually assimilated, and the French Chapel eventually closed in 1787.

22. William Brodrick, painted in 1614.

THE BRODRICKS

The Brodricks, lords of the manor of Dunsford from 1664 to the present, rose in four generations from citizen of London with a house and a few acres in Wandsworth to a Viscountcy and vast estates in Ireland. The first in Wandsworth was William Brodrick, who had come from Richmond in Yorkshire to London before 1587 and established himself as an embroiderer. By 1605 he had purchased a house in Putney Bridge Road and a few acres elsewhere in Wandsworth. In 1607 he became Embroiderer to King James I. He was buried in London in 1621, though his wife, Margaret, had been buried in Wandsworth.

The family's rise really began with the marriage of William's son Thomas to Katherine Nicholas, probably in about 1620. The marriage brought connections with the powerful Villiers, Hyde, Apsley and St John families. Thomas was knighted in 1625, and by 1633 was occupying a newly-built house on the site of the Savage Farm, just north of the church. He died in 1641.

His eldest son, Alan, then aged nineteen, became involved in the dangerous world of royalist intrigue through his family connection with Edward Hyde, later Earl of Clarendon. Alan was secretary to the Royalist organisation known as the Sealed Knot, transmitting intelligence to and from the Royalists in Holland and France. In 1659 he was imprisoned in the Tower of London, but following the Restoration of Charles II in 1660 he was knighted, appointed Surveyor General of Ireland and granted extensive lands in County Cork. In 1664 he purchased the manor of Dunsford (though not its enclosed lands in the south or the Garratt estate), and for a few years Wandsworth had a resident lord of the manor. He also obtained other Wandsworth property, including the former mansion of the Wilfords (on the site now occupied by the western part of the Arndale Centre).

Samuel Pepys recorded that Brodrick and his cousin Alan Apsley once held up business in the House of Commons for half an hour by speaking while drunk, and Brodrick himself later stated that 'it was a Pagan and abandoned way he sometimes pursued'. A severe illness two years before his death brought about repentance, after which he

regularly attended church and read the Psalms. He died, unmarried, in 1680, and was buried in the new family vault in All Saints Church.

His Wandsworth estates passed to his nephew Thomas, and in 1730 to *his* nephew Alan, Viscount Midleton. The latter also inherited family property at Peper Harow near Godalming, and from 1730 the family's connection with Wandsworth was as absentee landlords. Nevertheless, they retained a strong attachment to the place where the dynasty had been established: as late as 1836 the fourth Viscount Midleton was buried in All Saints Church, and when the ninth Viscount was elevated to Earl Midleton in 1920 he took the subsidiary title of Viscount Dunsford of Dunsford.

WRITERS AND ARTISTS
Seventeenth-century Wandsworth had several out-of-the-ordinary residents. One was Francis Lodowick (1619-94), son of a merchant and Protestant refugee from Flanders. By 1657 he occupied houses both in London and Wandsworth, where

23. A seventeenth-century house on North Side, at the north-west corner of the Common.

he was a vestryman. Lodowick traded abroad in cloth and books, and described himself as a 'mechanic' rather than a scholar, but he was well-read and wrote extensively. He was a friend of Samuel Hartlib, Robert Hooke and John Aubrey, and was elected a Fellow of the Royal Society in 1681. His works included a system of universal characters which could represent words in any language.[14]

Dr William Aglionby (died 1705) acquired a small house by the Thames in Bridge Field, east of the windmill there, in 1681, but stayed only a few years. He was a physician, Fellow of the Royal Society, traveller and diplomat.[15]

Richard Steele, later (with Addison) publisher of the *Tatler* and the *Spectator*, stayed briefly at Wandsworth in 1701 in order to obtain the peace and quiet to write his first play, a successful comedy entitled *The Funeral: or Grief à-la-Mode*. His land-lady taught girls to read and make bone-lace, and he noted that 'some of her scholars are a little too

tall to be looked at with indifference'. He spent his evenings drinking with a local miller.[16]

John Bushnell, the sculptor, bought a house and workshop in Bridge Field, next to the windmill, in 1677, and retained them until his death in 1701, although by the late 1680s he no longer occupied them. Bushnell returned from abroad after the Restoration with advanced ideas of the Baroque style. He considered himself better than any other sculptor in England, but was disappointed in his hopes of royal patronage. Among his surviving works are monuments to Samuel Pepys's wife Elizabeth in St Olave, Hart Street, Lord Mordaunt in Fulham Church, Edward Wynter in Battersea Church and Sir Thomas and Lady Katherine Brodrick at Peper Harow. In later life Bushnell was increasingly unbalanced, and his two sons (equally eccentric) smashed up his remaining work because they said he had never been properly appreciated.[17]

24. *A large house of great but indeterminate age on the western corner of Garratt Lane and the High Street, seen in 1863. This may be the earliest surviving photograph of Wandsworth. The house was Chapman's academy in the 1790s, and was demolished in about 1866.*

25. A view of Wandsworth from the east in 1750 (from close to the present Wandsworth Town Station). Fairfield Street is in the foreground; ahead are All Saints Church, with Church Row in front of it, and the Middle Mill with its windmill.

Georgian Wandsworth

Wandsworth grew rapidly in the eighteenth and early nineteenth centuries, its population rising from perhaps 2100 in 1700 to 4554 in 1792[1] and 7614 in 1841. The village became much more densely built up, with several alleys being constructed off the High Street and the Plain. A number of brick houses from the eighteenth century still exist, such as the house now belonging to Young's Brewery, erected by John Porter, bricklayer in 1724,[2] 22-24 Putney Bridge Road and Wandsworth House on East Hill, as well as many smaller houses. The finest survivor is Church Row, built on land acquired by Peter Paggen in 1717 and completed in 1718 (despite the date 1723 on the sundial). There were six houses (Nos. 7 to 9 being added later), each of three storeys with three rooms per floor and gardens running down to the Wandle.[3]

The hamlet of Garratt had grown by 1787, but there was little subsequent development there. In 1851 virtually all its inhabitants were labourers. Summerstown is first mentioned, as Summer's Town, in 1801, and was recognisably a hamlet by

1838, with 35 small houses. The occupations recorded in the 1851 census suggest that it grew up mainly to accommodate workers at the copper mill and the textile printing works just over the parish boundary in Wimbledon, and at least ten of the cottages were built in about 1808 by Benjamin Paterson, who was both a farmer and the manager of the copper mill.[4] The intention may have been to ensure that the workers did not become a charge on Wimbledon parish.

By the late 1760s Wandsworth had an annual fair, held in a field east of Fairfield Street and south of where the railway now runs. It lacked any legal authority, but survived an attempt to suppress it in 1771, when it was claimed that 'players of interludes and other evil disposed persons had ... built booths and sheds' used for plays and gaming, 'which had manifestly tended to the encouragement of vice and immorality'. That year people departed early instead of 'staying drinking and committing outrages and disorders til two or three in the morning'. In the 1820s the fair was on Whit Monday for cattle and the following Tuesday and Wednesday for 'toys and pleasure'. It was finally suppressed in the early 1830s.[5]

EARNING A LIVING

After the 1670s, the next overall view of occupations is provided by the censuses of 1841 and 1851.

26. *A row of eighteenth-century dwellings almost on the corner of West Hill and Putney Bridge Road, part of which survives.*

27. *Church Row, Wandsworth Plain, completed in 1718.*

The main changes by 1851 were the increased proportion serving the needs of the town itself (building, food, clothing etc – from 23% to 47%), the great decline in the proportion of watermen (from 14% to 3%) and the increased proportion involved in road transport (from 4% to 8%), including carmen, coachmen, draymen, blacksmiths, wheelwrights, carters and grooms. Agriculture, including gardening, still accounted for 13% (compared with 20% in the 1670s), though some of the

9% who were labourers will also have worked on the land. 18% had industrial occupations, including those in the mills and in crafts such as basket-making and coach-making (compared with 23% in the 1670s), but this probably reflected recent decline in some of the long-established industries. The most numerous industrial workers were then the brewers, maltsters and distillers (36 heads of household), millers (30), engineers and millwrights (24) and papermakers (21).

Of those still working on the river, twelve were described as watermen, fifteen as lightermen and eight as fishermen, together with six working on wharves. However, in 1801 the Curate had noted 'about 100 persons fishermen, & their apprentices, who were at this time down the river, far below Bridge, & who perhaps do not return home above once in a month or six weeks'.[6]

ENCLOSURE CONTROVERSY

Much of the parish continued to be farmed from the village, the old manor house sites of Dunsford and Allfarthing and the Garratt farm, but several new farms had appeared elsewhere by the 1740s – Howit's or Hewitt's Farm on the north side of West Hill, Burntwood Farm opposite Garratt Green and Bagley's Farm in the south-east corner of the parish. In 1723, James Lidgould at Dunsford Farm had 328 sheep and lambs, twenty hogs, seven

28. *Waterside, seen from the Thames in 1852. These houses were slightly west of the Ship pub. Waterside tended to be occupied by watermen and fishermen.*

29. *One of the views enjoyed from villas on East Hill, looking eastwards across Bridge Field towards St Paul's Cathedral. On the left is apparently the Jews House, and to its right the windmill in Bridge Field.*

30. *James's Yard, set back from the High Street on the west bank of the Wandle. The site was later used for the swimming baths and is now part of the Arndale Centre.*

cows, nine cart horses, 69 acres of crops, especially wheat, turnips and savoys, stocks of grain, peas and beans, 412 loads of hay and straw and a large amount of dung (worth £240).[7]

There were about 150 acres of market-garden ground in 1809, and twenty acres were used by Mr Rigge, a perfumer in Bond Street, for lavender and rose trees. The market-gardens were scattered around the parish, and included a substantial part of Bridge Field, where the gardeners were among the keenest on enclosure. The gardeners landed the dung on which their crops depended at a wharf by the Ship pub.[8]

When a survey was made of Wandsworth's 633 acres of open fields in 1706, 'for the preventing of many disputes & quarrels', there were 613 separate strips, in which just over a hundred people had an interest.[9] The obstacles to enclosure included both the large number of owners and the attitude of the Vestry, which, perhaps because of the complicated structure of manors, increasingly sought to regulate what was really the manors' business. In 1737 it began a policy of defending the open fields 'according to the ancient custom of this parish for the cattle belonging to the parishioners to graze therein in common'. As defined in 1739, these rights extended from the time the corn was cut and removed until 2nd November, disregarding any crops other than corn, and also applied to several of the meadows from 1st August to 2nd February. Otherwise the holders of the land could do as they wished.

In the 1780s, despite objections, the Vestry began to authorise enclosures of open field land in return for rent paid to the parish. In 1782 it was willing to acquiesce in an enclosure bill ending common grazing rights provided the parish received twenty acres in addition to the six already held. The scheme failed, as did another in 1800.[10] In fact, the rights exercised by the Vestry, though long-established, were unusual and highly dubious: the Vestry was not the proprietor of the soil, and grazing rights belonged to copyholders holding land from the manors, not to 'parishioners'. Nevertheless, some of the Vestry's enclosure rents continued to be paid until 1851.[11]

Another attempt at enclosure was made by Earl Spencer and others in 1828, covering both Wandsworth and Battersea. 473 acres of open fields then remained in Wandsworth. The promoters stated that 'This minute subdivision of property, and the custom of turning out ... most seriously affect the value of these fields. Of necessity they cannot be properly drained, nor can they be cultivated in the most advantageous manner, and the crops are liable to depredations of all kinds'; they were worth little more half the value of enclosed lands, and parts would increase tenfold in value if enclosed and used for the most suitable purpose (presumably market-gardening). The public, they claimed, had no right to walk over such fields, and yet 'there has been ... as much said in favour of the public on this occasion as if the lands to be inclosed had been a cricket ground or a bowling green, and exclusively devoted to public amusement'.[12]

The Bill was fiercely opposed, partly because it was regarded as a precursor to enclosure of the commons (which the promoters had originally intended) and partly because enclosure was expected to cause a great increase in building and 'those buildings will be of so low a class as to burden the Parish with a needy and disorderly population'.[13] The Bill was defeated. The tithe map of 1838 still shows the open fields and their strips, but enclosure seems thereafter to have occurred piecemeal, and by 1865 the strips had gone, except a few where Wandsworth Park is now.

THE SPENCERS AND WIMBLEDON PARK

The Spencers became important locally in 1744, when John Spencer inherited Wimbledon Manor from his grandmother, Sarah, Duchess of Marlborough. They acquired the manors of Battersea and Wandsworth in 1763, Downe in 1792 and Allfarthing in 1816. Only Dunsford eluded them, just as it had the Westminster monks, though the Spencers acquired much of its land.

The Spencers made a major impact on the landscape by extending Wimbledon Park into the parish. John Spencer (later the first Earl Spencer)

was passionate about hunting and shooting, and therefore needed a large park. In 1758 he purchased much of the land of Dunsford Manor from the Duke of Bedford, added part of Wandsworth's West Common and enclosed 215 acres in Wimbledon Park. The whole park was landscaped by Capability Brown, who created the present lake. In or shortly before 1782 all of what remained of Wandsworth West Common up to Park Side and West Hill was added. The new park's eastern boundary was Merton Road; its northern boundary was close to Replingham Road, Combemartin Road and Beaumont Road. The Spencers and their visitors were delighted with the extended park: one wrote in 1780 that 'I did not think there could have been so beautiful a place within seven miles of London'. One of the keepers of the lodge in the north-west corner, Robert Tebbutt, gave his name to Tibbet's Corner.[14]

VOLTAIRE IN WANDSWORTH

Wandsworth's most distinguished resident in the eighteenth century was Voltaire (1694-1778), philosopher, leading figure of the Enlightenment and the most celebrated man in Europe. He came from France to England in May 1726, already a well-known writer, effectively as an exile following a quarrel with the Chevalier de Rohan. He stayed until late 1728, and spent much of the intervening time with Everard Fawkener in Wandsworth. He wrote in October 1726 that Fawkener, whom 'I had seen but once at Paris, carried me to his own country house, wherein I lead an obscure and charming life since that time, without going

31. One of the isolated farms – Burntwood Farm, north of Burntwood Lane opposite Garratt Green.

32. (Above) Voltaire in 1718, aged 24.

33. (Top right) Plan of 1758 for the enclosure of part of the West Common in the Spencers' Wimbledon Park. The two main roads shown are now the A3 and Wimbledon Park Side. The areas marked A to F were enclosed, extending the park from the old irregular boundary to a new one further west.

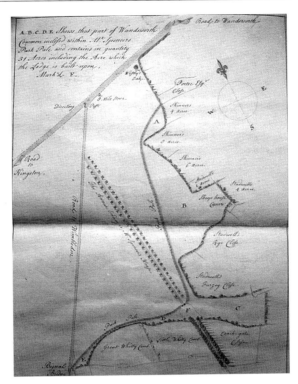

34. Sir Everard Fawkener, drawn by Jean Etienne Liotard in Turkey shortly after Fawkener's departure from Wandsworth.

to London, and quite given over to the pleasures of indolence and of friendship'.

Everard Fawkener (1694-1758) was a London merchant (a member of the Levant Company) and a scarlet dyer at Wandsworth. Where he lived in Wandsworth is not known for certain, but most of his property, including his dye works, later passed to the Williamson family,[15] and so their house, Albert House in Garratt Lane, may well have been his. He spent his leisure reading the classics and collecting ancient coins and medals.

Voltaire at first led a retired life in England, but later moved in the highest literary and scientific circles, corresponding with Swift, Pope and Bolingbroke. The master and teachers at Wandsworth's Quaker school helped teach him English.[16] After his return to France he and Fawkener, whom he described as 'the good and plain philosopher of Wandsworth', continued to correspond, and he dedicated his tragedy of *Zaire* to Fawkener in 1732. Fawkener left trade and Wandsworth in 1735: he was ambassador in Constantinople for seven years and then secretary to the Duke of Cumberland, whom he accompanied at the Battle of Culloden, as well as holding the lucrative office of joint post-master-general. He was described in 1745 as witty, unpretentious and open-hearted. He died in 1758.

The Wandsworth Mills

The first overall view of Wandsworth's mills is from 1610, when there were four – two between the Wandle bridge and the Thames and two above the bridge. In 1610, 40 quarters of corn, plus 67 for the King's use, were being ground every week at the Lower Mill, 60 at the Middle (or Brazil) Mill, 80 at the Upper Mill and 100 at Adkins Mill (the uppermost of the four).[1] Wheat was sent from Kingston and Brentford markets, the greater part of it on the account of bakers, chandlers and mealmen of London. These four mills may well have been the seven Domesday mills, since three of them were each described in the early seventeenth century as consisting of two mills – one of them more specifically as 'two mills under one roof'.

All Wandsworth's mills were corn mills in 1610, but this was unusual, for both before and after 1610 one or more of them was nearly always being used for other purposes. One had become a fulling mill by 1303, removing grease from cloth by pressing it with a slurry of water and clay. In 1376 the fullers of London complained that the 'hurers' of London (makers of shaggy fur caps) were fulling their caps at mills at Wandsworth and elsewhere, and that the mixing of caps with their cloths caused the cloths to be crushed and torn. Fulling of cloth apparently continued at Wandsworth until the sixteenth century, and there was again a fulling mill in 1624.[2]

The Wandle fell only about five feet between each of its mills (not quite three feet between Wandsworth's Adkins Mill and Upper Mill), so the mill wheels must have derived their power from the strength of flow rather than the fall of the water. Water supply on the Wandle was already a problem in 1610, when the practice was to pen up the water for six hours a day – longer in summer – to ensure sufficient flow when the mills were working.

The water-mills rapidly declined in importance in the second half of the nineteenth century as water extraction at Croydon caused falling water levels and alternative forms of power came into widespread use. Adkins Mill in 1813 was the first of several mills to acquire an auxiliary steam engine,[3] and some of the mills later used gas and electricity. The last use of water power in Wandsworth was at the Upper Mill, though only to

35. The north (downstream) side of the Middle Mill, drawn by Francis Grose in about the 1770s and seen from the Causeway, which leads in the bottom right-hand corner towards the Plain.

generate electricity for lighting and heat, and ceased in 1928.

In addition to the water mills, there were four windmills at various times. The earliest was in Waterside in 1633, but is not recorded again. The second had originally stood on Putney Heath, and was moved in the 1660s to the Thames-side in Wandsworth's Bridge Field (east of the present bridge) by George Buddle, who subsequently found the competition from water mills more intense than expected.[4] The third formed part of the Middle Mill by 1750. The fourth – the only survivor – on Wandsworth Common, was really a wind pump rather than a mill.

LOWER, MIDDLE AND UPPER MILLS

The Lower Mill, nearest the Thames, was the 'Lampetmille' in the sixteenth century, and was sometimes known later as Loam Pit Mill or Causeway Mill. In 1610 it had the specific task of grinding all the corn levied under the purveyance system in thirteen counties for supplying the King and court. By 1723 it was an oil mill, used to press oil from fatty vegetable seeds such as linseed. From 1745 it was operated by successive owners of the Battersea distillery, presumably for grinding malt. By 1788 Richard Bush, the Wandsworth distiller, held it, and, from 1826, Daniel Watney, a corn miller;[5] thereafter it remained a corn mill.

In 1853 the Lower Mill had three wheels. It was described in that year as a tidal mill, but seems to have suffered from rather than harnessed the tides, which then prevented it working from six to eight hours per day.[6] It went out of use in about 1893 and was demolished by 1898.

The Middle Mill was known by 1569 as the Brazil Mill – a reference to brazil wood, which was rasped in a mill to produce red and purple dyes. Dye-making had ceased by 1610, if not long before, but the name persisted for a time. The Middle Mill was the least powerful of Wandsworth's mills, and, perhaps for this reason, it had acquired a windmill by 1750. This was an unusual combination, since windmills are usually on higher ground. In 1804 it was reckoned that the water mill could drive four pairs of stones and the machinery for dressing flour and the windmill could drive two pairs of stones. The windmill had fallen out of use and lost its sails by 1825.[7] The Middle Mill was the only one of Wandsworth's mills which was a corn mill continuously from 1610, and it remained in use until about 1893.

The Upper Mill long retained its form as two mills under one roof, the two mills sometimes being part of different industries. By 1723 the east mill was a leather mill or skinning mill, and it was probably the offensive smells and waste it gave rise to which led the Vestry to prosecute the owner in 1723. The west mill was a copper mill by 1729, operated by John Appleby & Co from 1733 or earlier until the 1740s. After George Shepley rebuilt

36. The windmill which was moved from Putney Heath to Wandsworth in the 1660s, drawn by John William Edy in about 1798. It stood a little east of the present Wandsworth Bridge, and disappeared early in the nineteenth century. To its left is one of the gunpowder houses.

37. *The south side of the Lower Mill, seen from the Causeway in about 1890. It stood just south-west of the present Causeway Bridge, on the site now occupied by an electricity substation. The building shown here was probably constructed following the fire which destroyed the Lower Mill in 1777.*

38. *The Middle Mill, seen from the south end of the Causeway. Armoury Way now runs between where the photographer is standing and the site of the mill. The building shown here was probably of the mid-eighteenth century, as it is known to have been rebuilt by Mr Tealing prior to 1770.*

the mill in 1770-1, the east part remained an oil mill, while the west part was used as a corn mill. The engineer, John Smeaton, may have been in charge of the rebuilding, since there are drawings of his relating to Shepley's mill at around that time and he conducted experiments designed to make the best possible use of the small head of water available. His plan of 1789 shows the mill as having two internal wheels and a separate smaller wheel for driving the flour-dressing plant.[8]

The mills passed to Daniel Watney by 1817, and were rebuilt in brick as a corn mill in 1818,[9] remaining a corn mill thereafter. A building which existed over its bypass channel by 1838 was probably an additional mill. In 1840 James Watney and his partner Henry Wells were working 31 pairs of stones at the Middle and Upper Mills, and fewer than 50 employees, supported by 26 work horses and ten or twelve nags, prepared and distributed flour for 50,000 people.[10]

By 1898 the Upper Mill, managed by Bulstrode, Pimm & Co, depended on electricity and gas rather than water power, and the grain was crushed between steel rollers instead of millstones. The firm manufactured 'Wando bread', into which

40. *The Old Mill House, apparently of seventeenth-century date, close to the Middle Mill on the east side of the Plain. It was said to be in a dangerous condition in 1924, and was probably demolished soon afterwards.*

39. *The Upper Mill in about 1885, seen from the east. 33 employees are assembled – draymen, office workers, a maintenance man with an oil can and mill workers in white overalls. The clock and the shadows indicate that it is 7.25 am.*

41.   *Part of the Upper Mill (probably an additional mill) erected over the mill's bypass channel before 1838. It was not demolished until 1962.*

some of the wheat germ removed when preparing the flour for white bread was reintroduced, improving its flavour and nutritional value. The main Upper Mill building, recently re-equipped, was destroyed by fire in 1928, throwing twenty men out of work,[11] and this brought to an end at least 850 years of flour milling in Wandsworth.

ADKINS MILL

Adkins Mill, just south of Mapleton Road, was probably named after an early tenant. It is first recorded in 1363-4, when the Abbey repurchased the lease from Roger Finch, vintner of London, the first of many Londoners recorded owning Wandsworth mills. It had the most varied industrial career of any of Wandsworth's mills, and was almost certainly the medieval fulling mill. In 1610 it was a corn mill, but by 1654 it had become a copper mill, in which copper was beaten into plates and other forms by water-driven hammers.

It was leased in that year to four London armourers. The mill was actually managed by Nicholas Lesow, then aged 22 and variously described as a batterer and a forger, who was paid

42.   *George Pimm, manager of the Upper Mill from 1862 and joint-owner from 1875 until his death in 1885. He was one of the most advanced and enterprising millers in England, renowned in the trade for his introduction of continental mechanical innovations.*

fixed prices per hundredweight for hammering 'bowles' into plates and 'kettells'. Copper and coal were brought from London by water, and copper was sent back to London in the same way. In 1661 part of the mill was let to Henry Chinnall, a corn miller, providing another example of two industries sharing a mill.[12] The family of one of the partners of 1654, Henry Robinson, eventually gained control of the mill and retained it until at least 1762;[13] they several times held the Mastership of the Company of Armourers and Brasiers.

In 1777 the lease was taken over by James Henckell the younger, an iron forger.[14] Henckell pulled down 'the ancient works' and created a more extensive business on the site. There were plenty of iron works around London, but Henckell's undertook a wider range of processes and was probably unique in the London area. It did not produce iron from ore, but it did make wrought iron from pig iron, and this was then forged with a water-powered hammer and used in the manufacture of cannon and other items.

In 1813 Hughson wrote that 'At these mills are cast shot, shells, cannon, and other implements of war; in another part of it the wrought iron is manufactured, and the great effect of mechanic power is exemplified in all their operations; in the splitting of iron bars of prodigious length; in a pair of shears which will cut asunder pieces of iron more than two inches in thickness; and in the working of a hammer, which weighs from five hundred and a half to six hundred pounds'. Sir Richard Phillips in about 1816 enthused about 'the colossal powers of the welding hammer, the head of which, though a ton in weight, gives a stroke per second; the power of shears, which cut thick bars of iron like threads; the drawing out of iron hoops by means of rollers, and the boring of cannon ... all of which I saw going on at the same instant, without bustle or effort'.[15]

According to Phillips, 'On my remarking to the proprietor of this foundry, that the men mingled themselves with the fire like salamanders; he told me, that, to supply the excessive evaporation, some of them found it necessary to drink eight or ten pots of porter per day. Many of them presented in their brawny arms, which were rendered so by the constant exertion of those limbs; and in their bronzed countenances, caused by the action of the heat and the effluvia, striking pictures of true sons of Vulcan; and, except in occasional accidents, they enjoyed, I was told, general good health, and often attained a hearty old age'.

Iron mills did their work by 'sudden gushes or flashes of the water passing thro' the works of their mills with great violence', and Henckell

43. The Royal Paper Mills in about 1900, seen from the south-west (from what is now King George's Park).

proved particularly troublesome to his neighbours, penning up the water thirteen inches above the level agreed by his predecessors and releasing it in great surges, causing difficulties for Mr Shepley's Upper Mills and Mr Gardiner's bleaching grounds downstream. Moreover, Henckell, 'from the profits of his mill ... can afford to pay costs of one or two actions every year'.[16] How this was resolved is unclear, but one remedy may have been the creation of a larger millpond and a new reservoir for the Upper Mill.

Henckell's business continued under George Day & Sons until at least 1832, though on a much-reduced scale. In 1836 the mill became Thomas Creswick's paper mill. Creswick is said to have supplied a large proportion of the London trade with playing cards, Bristol boards, drawing papers and tinted papers. Following Creswick's death in 1840 there was a succession of short-lived papermakers, many of whom became bankrupt. However, in 1854 the mill was taken over by William McMurray, a Glaswegian, and was henceforth known as the Royal Paper Mills. It was soon supplying a range of papers, including high-quality newsprint to *The Times* and the *Illustrated London News*. Much of the paper was made from esparto grass (or rush) imported from estates owned by McMurray in Spain and North Africa (hence the nearby Esparto Road). Water power was used to beat the material at various stages.[17]

Much of the mill was destroyed by fire in 1903, throwing 160 people out of work. It soon reopened, but had closed for good by 1909 and was demolished a year later. Water power has never again been used there, though the site has remained in industrial use.[18]

44. *Garratt Mill, rebuilt on a smaller scale as a bone mill in the late nineteenth century.*

THE GUNPOWDER MILL

Until the 1650s there were no mills in Wandsworth south of Adkins Mill. Garratt Mill, situated south-west of Earlsfield Station (at the end of Trewint Street), originated as James Lloyd's gunpowder mill in the 1650s or 1660s. Gunpowder manufacture involves mixing saltpetre, charcoal and sulphur, and at this period the mixture had to be forcibly compressed in a mill. Lloyd built four mills at Wandsworth in 1655 or 1656 (probably meaning four wheels under one roof) and then two more mills further upstream in 1661. The latter were on land known as Peasecroft, which suggests that they were the later Garratt Mill; Lloyd's other mills did not survive, and their site is unknown. Legal proceedings were taken against Lloyd by Edward Barker, whose iron mill in Wimbledon was affected by Lloyd penning up the water at his new mills, but Lloyd resisted this by enlisting the support of the Privy Council.[19]

In 1687 the Wandsworth mills were the second largest source of gunpowder in England. They were still operating in 1729, but the site is marked on Rocque's map of the early 1740s as 'Strong Mill', and Melancton Strong was later recorded as an oil miller there. It remained an oil mill until at least 1853.[20]

When Sir Richard Phillips visited the mill in about 1816, 'my attention was attracted by a pretty mansion, which pleased my eye, though the monotonous blows of its adjoining oil-mill annoyed my ear. The owner, Mr Were, politely exhibited its details; and more mechanical ingenuity than is here displayed could not well be applied to aid the simple operation of extracting oil from linseed. A magnificent water-wheel, of thirty feet, turns a main shaft, which gives motion to a pair of vertical stones, raises the driving-beams, and turns a band which carries the seed, in small buckets, from the floor to the hopper. The shock on the entire nervous system, produced by the noise of the driving-beams as they fall on the wedges, is not to be described'.[21] It is probably no coincidence that it was usually the mills further from the town which dealt with oil, iron and copper, not to mention gunpowder.

In the early 1860s Garratt Mill became a paper mill, and by 1873 it was a bone mill, turning animal bones into grease and crushed bone, used as fertiliser. It had been rebuilt on a smaller scale by 1894, and was demolished in about 1899.[22]

One other mill (discussed later) was established at Duntshill by 1865, but seems to have been small and short-lived.

45. *The yard of Young's Brewery in 1896.*

Working Lives

Wandsworth's industries were not confined to those carried on at the mills, though almost all were connected in some way with the Wandle and its water. There were industries related to those of the mills, such as the manufacture of bolting cloth; industries employing the Wandle water other than for power, such as dyeing and bleaching; and industries which found a Thames-side location convenient for bringing in raw materials or sending out their finished produce, such as distilling.

BREWING AND DISTILLING

The history of what is now Young's Brewery – the only survivor among the enterprises discussed in this chapter – can be traced back to 1576, when Humphrey Langridge, occupier of 'the Rame', was described as 'a beer brewer of Wandsworth'. The Langridge family's property later passed to the Cripps family, and the brewery was run by Edmund Cripps from 1639 or earlier and then successively by the two husbands of James Cripps' widow, Mary – Samuel White (d.1668) and Captain Somerset Draper (d.1675).[1]

By the time of Draper's arrival in 1670 the brewery was already a substantial enterprise. Mary Draper stated that Somerset Draper had made about £800 a year profit, and an inventory made in 1675 records not only large stocks of malt, hops and coal but also 'backs, tuns and casks great & small' worth £135, 'the copper as it hangs' (£135), eleven horses (£28) and three drays (£8).[2] The horses form a living link between the seventeenth century or earlier and the present; Young's undoubtedly has one of the oldest continuously-operated stables in the country.

Since 1670, three families have owned the brewery. The Drapers retained it until 1763. Thomas Tritton, wine merchant, brewer and banker at Ashford in Kent, bought the brewery in 1763, and after his death his son George ran it until his own death in 1831. It was then purchased by Charles Allen Young and his partner Anthony Fothergill Bainbridge. Young, then aged 44, had connections in the brewing industry through a business mak-

46. *The heart of Young's Brewery prior to the 1980s: the coppers of 1869 (on the right) and 1885 (on the left), seen in the 1920s.*

47. *Wandsworth Distillery from the Thames in 1832 (watercolour by S.H. Prosser).*

48. Drays in the distillery yard in about 1900.

ing backs (shallow vats used both in brewing and dyeing). The Youngs have retained control of the brewery ever since, and the present chairman, John Allen Young, is the fifth generation of Youngs in charge of the firm.[3]

In 1832, five months after Young and Bainbridge's takeover, much of the brewery was destroyed by fire, but it was soon rebuilt. In 1835 they installed the first of two beam engines manufactured by James Wentworth of Wandsworth, the second being added in 1867. Both remain in working order today, though no longer in regular use. The tun room was rebuilt after another fire in 1882, and the present chimney was built in 1908. Increasing demand led to the construction of a new brewhouse in 1984.[4] Though now a public company, Young's remains a family business, and the prestige of its product is probably higher now than at any time in its history.

Wandsworth's other substantial brewery, the Union Brewery by the Thames on the east side of Point Pleasant, lasted only from about 1820 to 1920. At least three malthouses existed in the nineteenth century, and possibly a distillery in the late seventeenth century, but the other major enterprise in the drinks trade was the distillery by the Thames in the north-east corner of the parish. It was built by Richard Bush in about 1790, and by 1850 belonged to John Watney & Co. In the 1880s it had about 70 employees. It closed in 1989.[5]

FRYING PANS AND KETTLES

John Aubrey wrote in the late seventeenth century that 'At Wansworth is a manufacture of brass plates, for kettles, skellets, frying-pans, &c. by Dutch men, who keep it as a mystery'. This manufacture took place at Point Pleasant, beginning in about 1634, and was on a considerable scale. In the hearth tax list of 1665, against fourteen names with hearths (or chimneys) ranging in number from one to five is the following note: 'These be the fryinge pan houses they have but one or 2 Chimneys apeece the others are forges ... they are all Dutchmen'. The parish register describes the workers as 'batterers'. Their houses and forges were on the west side of Point Pleasant towards the north end, and there was a warehouse by the Thames on the east side.[6]

Their landlord was Edward Barker, who was almost certainly responsible for bringing them to England and may himself have been Dutch. In his warehouse at Wandsworth in 1671 was a stock of frying pans, dripping pans, chafing dishes, plate iron and merchant iron valued at £1332, indicating about 80 tons of iron in stock. His will refers to his 'working tooles bellowes weights beames and scales and all goeing geeres whatsoever belonging to my plate mills workhowses and fforges' in Surrey, Somerset and Bristol. In Wandsworth, Barker owned the land and provided the raw material, paid the Dutchmen for the articles they produced and marketed the produce. The dozens of brasiers and ironmongers listed as debtors in his inventory, mostly in London, indicate that he supplied a large part of the London trade. Barker was also a major arms dealer during the Civil Wars: in 1644 he was the main supplier of arms and ammunition to the Eastern Association and thus to Cromwell, and in 1649 he supplied firearms for the expedition to Ireland.[7]

The iron mill on the Wandle just across the parish boundary in Wimbledon was established at about the same time as the forges at Point Pleasant and by 1660 if not earlier was operated by Barker, who used it to make 'armour plate and other iron plate'. The two sites were effectively a single enterprise: the Wimbledon mill provided the power for hammering iron bars into plates, whereas Point Pleasant had the Thames-side location for bringing in coal to provide heat for forging the plates into frying pans and kettles. Such skill was required to regulate the heat applied to the plates and to choose from the twenty or more different hammers used that there were only two master frying-pan makers in the whole country, at Wandsworth and at Newcastle-under-Lyme, the latter manufacture having apparently been established from Wandsworth.[8]

At least one of Barker's workmen listed in 1665 prospered at Wandsworth. In 1681 the churchwardens set up an inscription stating that 'Nicholas

49. *Williamson's dyeing works, on the east bank of the Wandle a little north of the present Mapleton Road, drawn by J.E. Nicholls in 1860-1.*

Tonnet having lived in ... Wandsworth about fifty years, and by his hard labour and good husbandry with God's blessing gathered together a considerable sum of money' gave the churchwardens £200, the interest to benefit him during his life and thereafter the poor of Wandsworth. They added that he was a French Protestant.[9]

Barker and his workmen seem to have used only iron; brass manufacture apparently came later. By 1712 the iron mill had become a copper mill, and by 1719 John Essington, a copper merchant, owned both the frying pan houses and a share in the former iron mill. In 1754 a traveller noted that 'They have a manufacture here of brass plates for making vessels', but in 1771 the frying pan houses passed to Messrs Gatty and Waller, chemists, and this presumably marks the end of the frying pan works.[10]

DYEING, BLEACHING AND CALICO-PRINTING

Like the other Wandle parishes, Wandsworth became a notable centre of the textile-finishing industries. At least two dyers had property in Wandsworth in the early 1550s.[11] However, no dyers are recorded subsequently until the 1650s, and then all with foreign names, suggesting that the industry had been re-established using new techniques from the Low Countries, particularly for scarlet dyeing.

The first of these was Nicholas Pluyme, scarlet dyer, mentioned in 1651. More is known about another dyer, Abraham Hebert, recorded at Wandsworth from 1654. Hebert was described as a Dutchman, though he signed the Huguenot petition in 1682 and left money in his will to the French Church in London. In 1682 he provided in his will that his grandson Abraham Gosselin was to have the use of his dwelling at Wandsworth 'with the dyhouse kettles tenters and appurtenances' for ten years. His executors' accounts indicate that two of the main activities were dyeing of stockings and dyeing of West Country serges (sent by Matthew Hebert from Exeter). Another dyer was Christian Loat, again with a foreign-sounding name, recorded at Wandsworth from 1665. An inventory made in 1682 records his '2 great kittells', barrels of copperas, crematorter and cochineal, a cart, three horses and four tenters (frames for cloths to be stretched on).[12]

Once established, the same sites tended to continue in use. Hebert's was close to Adkins Mill, and was almost certainly the site between the Wandle and Garratt Lane a little north of the present Mapleton Road, which was definitely a dyeworks by the 1720s. It later belonged successively to William Kirby, Snelling and Fawkener and the Williamson family, apparently closing in about 1830.[13] The only other dye-works which continued into the nineteenth century was on the east side of the Wandle north of the High Street (now part of Young's Brewery). This was in use by 1724 by Edward Applegarth, scarlet dyer; from 1765 until about 1830 it was used by members of the Barchard family.[14] There was also at least one dye-works west of the Wandle in the eighteenth century, and several tenter grounds are recorded by the Thames.

Although the continuous history of industrial dyeing in Wandsworth ends in about 1830, More Close Bleach and Dye Works, west of Garratt Green, is shown on maps from 1864 to the 1890s and Messrs Ellwood were dyeing furs in Frogmore from 1885.

Bleaching was introduced to England by the Dutch, and was being carried on in Mitcham by 1620. The first Wandsworth bleaching ground was established by Richard Pillett in 1657, between the Wandle and Garratt Lane south of Adkins Mill, for carrying on the 'trade of whiteing lynnen cloth'. By 1687 another bleaching ground was being worked by John Ousley south of the village, on the sidewater of the Wandle about where Broomhill Road and Buckhold Road now meet.[15] The bleaching process was later described as follows:

'The cloth was washed in ley made from wood ashes, then rinsed and afterwards spread out over the grass in the meadows. The flat meadows by the Wandle ... were divided into strips of grass by ditches. The calico was spread on the grass, and the men walking along the edge of the ditches by means of scoops skilfully drenched the calico. The action of the sun caused the calico to become white in about a month's time, if the weather were favourable.'[16]

Calico-printing was almost certainly brought to Wandsworth by the Huguenots, for the first two recorded at Wandsworth were Jean Bergeret and Rowland Bouchet in 1691,[17] though there were apparently no Huguenot owners of calico-printing works. Calicoes were cotton fabrics imported from India, and patterns were printed on them using wooden blocks or, later, metal plates. No power was required except by printers who used the rolling process available from the 1770s.

Calico-printing was closely associated with bleaching and, given the requirement for flat low-lying ground to create ditches and the labour of creating them, the two trades were even more tenaciously linked to specific sites than dyeing.

50. The landscape of bleaching and calico-printing: Mr Gardiner's estate in 1828, with the characteristic channels from which water was scooped over the cloth. The area shown is south of the High Street and between Merton Road and the Wandle; the bleaching grounds are now part of King George's Park. The first bleaching works was west of the Wandle's sidewater, where Down Lodge's outbuildings are shown on this plan (Broomhill Road originated as its approach). In the later eighteenth century the works moved to Frogs Island (to the north-east of the plan between the rail-road and the sidewater), and it closed shortly before this map was drawn.

Pillett's bleaching ground passed to John Page, who by 1729 was a calico printer. John Aldridge erected a new calico-printing works there at great expense in about 1825, but went bankrupt in 1828, when bleaching and calico-printing finally ceased on the site.[18] Ousley's was occupied by 1744 by David Asterley, calico-printer, and later became the largest industrial enterprise in the parish: in 1792, under Henry Gardiner, it employed 250 hands, as many as all Wandsworth's other manufactures put together. Its buildings included printing shop, painting and pencilling shop, glazing shop 'with drawing rooms over', mill house, dye house, blue dye house and copper plate shop. The works apparently closed in about 1820.[19]

Another site, in existence under Messrs Coleman & Co by 1776, straddled the Wimbledon/Wandsworth boundary west of Summerstown, where Riverside Road meets the Wandle.[20] The works was in Wimbledon parish, but the land in Wandsworth south of the present Garratt Park and Maskell Road was used as bleaching grounds by 1787.

Bleaching and calico-printing along the Wandle declined in the first half of the nineteenth century because of the use of chlorine for bleaching, together with increased use of machinery and steam power. However, some printing continued, particularly at Anthony Heath's Garratt Print Works (formerly Coleman & Co's) on the southern border of the parish, where engraved copper plates and printing presses were used. In 1850 this was the last such firm in Surrey, and employed about 40 men and six boys; it was still in business in 1871.[21] Two shawl printers are also recorded in Wandsworth in 1867.

OTHER INDUSTRIES

The Huguenots introduced hatmaking and feltmaking. Many of them had come from Caudebec, near Rouen in Normandy, a centre for furriers and the manufacture of felt and beaver hats, and they were later said to have had a secret liquid used in the preparation of rabbit and hare skins and beaver fur. The manufacture still existed on a reduced scale in 1792, when Mr Chatting, a grandson of one of the refugees, was a hatter.[22]

Another Huguenot industry was leather. The skinning mill, part of the Upper Mills, was run by Jacob Pappineau in 1726. Isaac Colon had a tanyard, for turning skins into leather, in the grounds of Downe Manor House in 1705. The next stage was the dressing of leather, and Josias Senne, one of the Huguenot petitioners of 1682, who had premises north of the High Street between the Wandle and the brewery, was recorded as a leather-dresser in 1687.[23]

51. Blackmore's bolting-cloth factory, on the west side of the Plain on a site now part of Armoury Way, in about 1898. There were six large wooden looms on the upper floor, where all the internal walls had been removed. Until 1882 it had been a handsome house with a high roof and five dormer windows.

Bolting cloths, used in mills to separate fine and coarse flour, were originally made with seams, which obstructed the process and wore out quickly, but in 1783 Benjamin Blackmore patented a loom for making cloths without seams. They were made first at Exeter, but the business moved to Wandsworth by 1789, and to a site on the west side of the Plain in 1814. The Wandsworth factory was believed to be the only one in the world. It closed after a long decline in about 1919.[24]

Of the several engineering works, the most notable was that of James Wentworth, in Dormay Street, founded in about 1816.[25] Its speciality was beam engines, such as the two which survive in Young's Brewery. It closed in about 1890.

Joseph Gatty and William Waller, chemists and druggists from London, leased the frying pan premises at Point Pleasant from 1771, and operated there as vinegar merchants. However they also supplied the chemical requirements of the dyers and calico-printers. In 1777 their buildings at Point Pleasant included an 'iron liquor house' and a 'madder stove and mill house' (madder being a plant yielding a red dye), and in 1814 the firm was described as preparing iron liquids and sours (acids) for calico-printers. It closed in about 1820.[26]

The least welcome industry was gunpowder storage. William Taylor erected a gunpowder warehouse in North Field in 1743, and at least one more towards the east of Bridge Field in 1748. Taylor was a ship chandler in Wapping, which indicates what the gunpowder was for, but the reason for choosing Wandsworth to store it is unknown. He built a dock 70 feet long west of Point Pleasant for shipping the gunpowder. The Vestry described the gunpowder houses as 'a teror to all the inhabitants', and contributed £50 towards a prosecution, but they still existed in the 1820s, and the two eastern ones were still there in 1838.[27]

52. *The Surrey Iron Railway wharf on the Cut in about the 1820s, seen from towards the north end of the present Ram Street. In the background on the left is the Lower Mill. This is the only known view showing the railway in operation.*

The Surrey Iron Railway

The Wandle's strong flow and the existence of so many mills made it useless for navigation, and yet the mills and other works needed transport for heavy goods. In 1799 a group of mainly Wandsworth industrialists sought the advice of William Jessop, the leading canal engineer. Jessop reported in 1799 that a canal from Wandsworth to Croydon (intended as the first part of a canal to Portsmouth) was impracticable unless the water which fed the Wandle could be used. He suggested instead an iron railway, which would be 'not much inferior' to a canal.

The result has rightly been called the world's first public railway. Previous lines had been intended for use by their owners, usually to connect coal mines and canals, rather than being

53. William Jessop (1745-1814), canal, dock and tramroad engineer, the engineer for the Surrey Iron Railway.

available for a toll to anyone who wished to convey goods along them. The Surrey Iron was also the first railway *company* in the world and the first railway sanctioned by Parliament independently of a canal.

A committee including Jessop and several Wandsworth industrialists first made a nine-day tour in and around Derbyshire to look at existing railways. They reported back enthusiastically. The Act was obtained in 1801 and work proceeded quickly. The eight-mile double-track line began

at a dock constructed just east of the Wandle in Wandsworth, capable of holding 30 barges, and proceeded via Summerstown and Mitcham to Croydon. In Wandsworth there were short branches to the Shepleys' warehouses west of the Wandle by Bell Creek (apparently constructed in 1806), to the Upper Mills and to the Garratt oil mill (on the line of Trewint Street).[1] The line was less important to Wandsworth businessmen than to those further from the Thames, but they were nevertheless major investors in it.[2]

In January 1802 'the first barge entered the lock, amidst a vast concourse of spectators, who rejoiced in the completion of this part of the important and useful work'. The northern part of the railway opened in late 1802, although the official opening was not until July 1803. Later a separate company extended the line southwards to the stone quarries at Merstham, but the proposal of 1802 for a link to London was not pursued.

The Surrey Iron Railway was too early to benefit either from steam locomotives (all its waggons were horse-drawn) or from wrought-iron rails (it used easily-broken cast-iron ones instead). Users of the line usually provided their own horses and waggons and paid a toll per ton carried per mile for use of the track, similar to the practice on

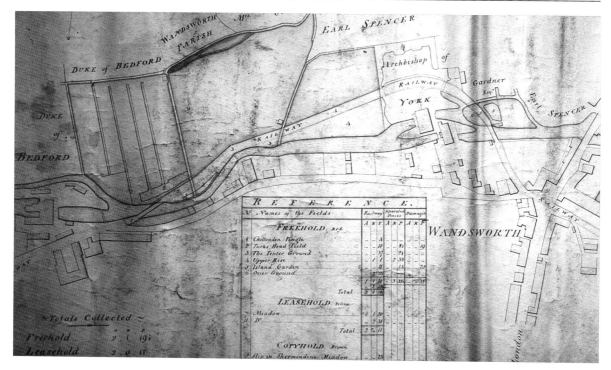

54. Part of a map of the Surrey Iron Railway in Wandsworth in 1801, extending from Wandsworth High Street on the right to Adkins Mill on the left. North is on the right. From Railway Wharf (out of view to the right), the railway passed along what is now Ram Street, crossed and re-crossed the Wandle (with a branch to the Upper Mill), briefly followed Garratt Lane, continued southwards beside Garratt Lane, crossed Little Garratt Green and passed along Summerstown. Only for very short stretches was it a street railway, and the reason for crossing the Wandle was probably because Garratt Lane was too narrow at that point.

turnpike roads. Usually the line was leased out for a fixed sum (James Lyon of Wandsworth being the lessee prior to 1845), but at several periods the company ran the line itself. The staff were a superintendent, a lockman (for the dock), a watchman and a man to repair the road (probably more than one repair-man in earlier days). Some of the traffic expected is indicated by the maximum tolls per ton-mile set out in the Company's Act: 2d for dung, 3d for other manures and building materials, 4d for metals, coal, corn, seeds, flour and malt, and 6d for other goods. Passengers were never carried, except at the line's formal opening.

The line undoubtedly contributed to the industrial development of the Wandle Valley. However, at the time of building there were some who doubted that it would ever pay, and they were proved right. The total dividends paid on the £120 shares, up to the last in 1825, amounted to only £10. 6s. 0d. The reasons appear to have been insufficient traffic and the cost of repairing easily-broken rails. Also, the track tended to become filled by dirt and stones, increasing the friction and thus reducing the benefit from using it. The completion of the Croydon Canal from Deptford to Croydon in 1809 diverted some of the traffic.

A series of water-powered mills was a much weaker basis for a railway than the coal mines which sustained most railways, especially as the railway connected the mills to the Thames and not to London itself. It might be worthwhile to convey heavy materials such as linseed oil by barge to Wandsworth and then rail, but sending out the finished product in that way involved transhipment twice – at Wandsworth into barges and at London into carts for final delivery – and for that purpose direct journeys by road-waggon were more efficient. In 1839 Croydon acquired a railway to London, and closure of the line from Croydon to Merstham in that year was said to have deprived the Surrey Iron of half its traffic. The line fell into increasing disrepair, and the rails from one track were used to repair the other. In 1845-6, one of the line's remaining users, an oil miller at Carshalton, was using one horse per waggon carrying two tons, only about three times as much as a horse could draw on the roads, whereas Jessop had indicated that horses could draw eight times as much on a railway as on a road.

In 1844 the Company made arrangements to sell the part of the line from Croydon to Allfarthing Lane to the Brighton Railway, which planned a steam-operated railway along the route, presumably swinging eastwards after Allfarthing Lane to meet the proposed Richmond Railway and have running powers to Waterloo. However, neither the sale nor the proposed line went ahead. The line's users in Wandsworth in its final year were James Watney, miller, George Lee, oil miller and James Lyon, wharfinger. The railway closed on 31 August 1846. The dock at Wandsworth, clearly the more successful part of the enterprise, outlasted the railway, and is discussed later. Part of the trackbed became the road now known as Ram Street,[3] one of the bridges over the Wandle apparently gave rise to Buckhold Road (now diverted), and some stone sleepers can be seen in the brewery wall in Ram Street, but otherwise no trace is left of the line.

56. A waggon on the Little Eaton Gangway near Derby. This was built in 1795 by Benjamin Outram, later engineer of the Surrey Iron Railway's sister railway, and gives a good idea of what the Surrey Iron Railway was like. The Surrey Iron's rails were about three feet long, and the flange to hold the rolling stock in place was part of the rail, whereas on later railways the flange forms part of the wheels. The rails were laid four feet two inches apart (slightly closer than the later standard gauge), on stone blocks about sixteen inches square and nine inches high.

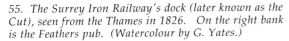

55. The Surrey Iron Railway's dock (later known as the Cut), seen from the Thames in 1826. On the right bank is the Feathers pub. (Watercolour by G. Yates.)

Villas and Mansions

Apart from West Hill, Wandsworth never acquired the aristocratic character of much of neighbouring Putney and Clapham parishes. The parting of the ways was probably the mid-seventeenth century, when Wandsworth embarked on its industrial career and a series of great houses was built in Putney and Roehampton. Although Wandsworth had eleven houses with ten or more hearths in 1664, Putney, a smaller parish, had twenty, and Wandsworth's largest, occupied by Sir Alan Brodrick, had fifteen hearths, whereas the largest in Putney parish had 57.[1]

In 1633, Wandsworth's larger houses were almost all in or around the village. The desire to escape the dirt and disease of the City, while remaining within easy reach of it, was probably the main reason for acquiring such places. Later, rather more was expected of a suburban retreat: pleasure grounds and seclusion, and if possible a fine view. Thus villas began to be built away from the village, especially on the higher ground of East Hill and West Hill, and some of the large houses in the village disappeared, such as the Brodricks' house and Downe Manor House. The grounds of the latter were being used for tanning, a notoriously smelly trade, by 1705.[2]

Many of Wandsworth's larger houses were not suburban retreats at all but were occupied either by schools or by local manufacturers. Several houses of the latter type survive, including Down Lodge in Merton Road, Wentworth House in Dormay Street and Prospect House in Point Pleasant. Most of the other large houses had disappeared by 1910.

EAST HILL AND AROUND THE COMMON

Large houses on the north side of East Hill included (from east to west) Wandsworth Manor House (discussed later); Elms Leigh, described in 1793 as 'a pleasant white house, which commands a western prospect over a beautiful grass plat'; East Hill House (north of Geraldine Road; demolished in 1909), described in 1793 as a modern house, commanding views to London, Hampstead

57. Prospect House, Point Pleasant, from the north in 1825, when it was occupied by Mr Gatty (watercolour by G. Yates). The house has recently been restored.

58. *(Above) The house of Sir James Sanderson, a Lord Mayor of London, on East Hill, drawn by John Charles Barrow in 1788. Melody Road replaced it in about 1891.*

59. *(Below) Wandsworth House, East Hill, in 1906, apparently of eighteenth-century date but possibly incorporating earlier work. The house is still standing, but has lost most of its front garden.*

and Harrow; and Wandsworth House, which is still there. On the south side, from east to west, were 'a lofty red brick house' occupied in 1793 by Sir James Sanderson, Lord Mayor of London (on the site of Melody Road); The Huguenots, inhabited by the Barchards at least from 1793 to 1851 (on the north-east corner of Geraldine Road); and the Lawn (replaced by Herndon Road in about 1887).

Bridge Field contained a few substantial houses, including Distillery House by the river (demolished in about 1903) and Jews House (later known as Bridgefield House) in York Road. The names of Jews House and Jews Row were derived from Jacob and Rachel Da Costa, who purchased a house and some land in Dunsford Manor in 1729. They died in 1760 and 1776 respectively.[3] The house appears to have pre-dated their purchase, and whether they ever occupied it is unknown. On the southern corner of York Road and Fairfield Street was the White House. There had been a house there since at least 1671, and it was described as a villa when the lawyer, George Gostling, a Proctor in Doctors Commons, purchased it in 1755. His attempts to assemble an estate around it illustrate the complications of Wandsworth land-ownership, with lands both copyhold and free-

60. *The Lawn, on the south side of East Hill (replaced by Herndon Road in about 1887).*

61. *Bridgefield House (formerly Jews House). It stood north-west of the junction of Jews Row and York Road, and was demolished in about 1865. This later drawing was presumably made from memory or from an earlier sketch.*

62. Francis Grose (c.1731-1791), antiquary and occupier of Mulberry Cottage (later The Gables) on North Side. He was the compiler of the Dictionary of the vulgar tongue *(1811), a compendium of slang.*

hold, in three manors, and most purchases including numerous scattered plots.[4]

On North Side, the most admired house was The Gables. The antiquary Francis Grose occupied it from at least 1764 to 1775. Much later it was the home of Clement Attlee's grandfather and his four daughters and one son (all unmarried). Attlee regarded it as an important part of his childhood, and described the dark dining room, with a window over the fireplace, upstairs rooms with sloping floors, deep window-seats and four-poster beds, the smoking room with swords and daggers on the wall and no carpets, and 'a large smoky garden'.[5] In an enclosure on the Common (now the northern part of Spencer Park) was a house occupied by Mr Wilson, who founded Price's Candle Factory at Battersea, and there were three or four substantial houses on West Side.

The group of large houses in the south-east part of the parish were relatively late arrivals, mostly of the early nineteenth century. The earliest was Wandsworth Lodge, in the extreme south-east corner (near where Trinity Road and Crockerton Road now meet), built by Richard Bush, son of the distiller, in the late eighteenth century. By 1836 it was occupied by Henry McKellar, who between then and his death in 1863 enclosed much of the southern part of Wandsworth Common. After his death the house was demolished and the 120-acre estate was built over.[6] Burntwood (demolished in about 1906) stood on the site of Burcote Road, and Burntwood Grange, Burntwood Lodge and Collamore were north of Burntwood Lane just west of the Common (the latter two being demolished in about 1914). Henry Perkins of Southwark, a wealthy brewer, purchased the farm east of Garratt Green in 1815 and built Springfield House there, but it was demolished in 1838 after the estate was purchased for Surrey's lunatic asylum.[7]

WANDSWORTH MANOR HOUSE

Wandsworth Manor House was not a manor house at all. It was built by Peter Paggen on land which he purchased in 1707, now where the underpass emerges north of East Hill. Paggen was of immigrant stock from the Low Countries, and between his first purchase in 1707 and his death in 1720 he acquired a substantial estate in Wandsworth. One ceiling in the house was painted with a portrait of Queen Anne, resulting in the legend that it had been built for the Queen, but the intertwined monograms of Peter and Catherine Paggen on the exterior confirm that it was built for them.[8] Paggen was an enthusiastic developer of his estate, for he also built Church Row.

Paggen's grandson sold the estate in 1759 to Matthew Blakiston, a wealthy City merchant, Lord Mayor of London in 1760 and later a baronet. Blakiston occupied the house for a time, but by the time of his death in 1784 it was leased out. It was then described as having a drawing room, dining room and parlour on the main floor, five bedrooms and two dressing rooms on the floor above, six attic bedrooms and household offices in the basement. There was stabling for nine horses, two coach houses, pleasure grounds, lawn and kitchen gardens.[9] In 1793 the house was occupied by Richard Bush, the distiller and miller, and was known as Swandown House. In its last years it was a ladies' boarding school, and it was demolished in 1891. Parts were incorporated in houses elsewhere, such as the portico and doorway at 78 Deodar Road, Putney.[10]

63. *Burntwood Grange, drawn by Edward Hassell in 1832, when newly-built and occupied by T. Anson. It was on the site of the present road of the same name, and was demolished in about 1940.*

64. *The hall and staircase of Wandsworth Manor House, showing the high quality of the carving. The staircase was later re-used elsewhere.*

65. *The garden front of Wandsworth Manor House in about 1890.*

66. *The front of the house built by Samuel Palmer (on the site of the present Orchard Estate), seen from the south in 1825 (watercolour by G. Yates).*

CENTRAL WANDSWORTH

The first house on the site west of Putney Bridge Road now occupied by the Orchard Estate was built by Samuel Palmer (1670-1738), an eminent surgeon, who practised in Great Tower Street in the City and was Treasurer of St Bartholomew's Hospital, President of St Thomas's Hospital and a Fellow of the Royal Society. He began buying property in Wandsworth in 1726. His estates passed in 1738 to his only child, Frances, who had married Peter Sainthill, her father's partner in the City surgery and a substantial landowner. An inventory made following Sainthill's death in 1775 indicates that the house was not especially large but was luxuriously furnished. On the ground floor were hall, great parlour, garden parlour and harpsichord parlour, and there were four main bedrooms (one called the tapestry room) and a dressing room on the first floor and four attic bedrooms. He had a coach and two horses. Sainthill was a man of wide interests, and left a large library and art collection.[11]

The estate passed to his grand-daughter Frances (known as Fanny), who at the age of seventeen married John Wilmot, a lawyer. Scandal followed. In early 1791, at Wandsworth and at their town house in Bedford Row, the 32-year old Fanny, mother of six children, committed adultery with the under-footman, Edward Washbourn, continu-

ing to visit him in his lodgings in Holborn after he had been dismissed. A lawyer acting for John Wilmot went to the Holborn lodgings, drilled holes in the wainscot and observed the guilty couple. The Wilmots' eight other servants (butler, coachman, footman, lady's maid, housekeeper, nursery-maid, housemaid and kitchen-maid) all gave evidence in the divorce proceedings. Following the divorce, Wilmot was legally entitled to all his wife's property, though he seems to have been generous to her. All the Wandsworth property was sold, the house being bought by Frederick Hahn, whose family kept it until the 1870s. In 1874 it was taken over by the Convent of the Sacred Heart, and in 1974 the Council bought it, demolished the buildings and built housing there.[12]

Just west of it was Putney Lodge, occupied until the 1880s by the merchant, Sigismund Rucker (now the site of the Library). Rucker's garden and his extensive hothouses (now the area from Santos Road to Schubert Road) were noted for beautiful and rare plants, especially orchids.[13] Nearby was the Sword House.

Garratt Lane boasted no particularly impressive houses, though there were several handsome ones belonging to manufacturers or millers, several of

which survived until the 1950s. Merton Road contained only Down Lodge, built in about 1783 by Henry Gardiner, the calico-printer, with a fine garden and extensive views over his bleaching grounds and beyond. Its occupants were usually proprietors of industrial enterprises, such as A.F. Bainbridge (partner in Young's Brewery) in 1838 and William Bulstrode the miller from 1897 to 1923. It survived a threat of demolition in 1994. The former Dunsford manor house further south had been only a farmhouse since the seventeenth century.[14] In Allfarthing Lane, part of the manor house, rebuilt since 1633 on a new site south of Allfarthing Lane and long occupied as a school, was said to have been incorporated in its successor, Elm Lodge.[15]

In Putney Bridge Road adjoining the boundary with Putney was Moliniere House, whose first known occupant was James Moliniere, a Huguenot, in the 1730s.[16] Its porch survives as part of the 1930s building on the site.

67. Earlsfield (formerly Elm Lodge), south-east of the junction of Allfarthing Lane and St Ann's Crescent, seen from around the present Barmouth Road in 1890. It was demolished in about 1891.

WEST HILL

West Hill began to be lined by substantial houses in the mid-eighteenth century. On the north side were the Clock House of about the 1760s, and Colebrook Lodge, built by Sir William Fordyce, a prominent physician, on land near Tibbet's Corner enclosed from the Common in 1764.[17]

The grandest house was the one which now forms part of the Royal Hospital for Neuro-Disability and was usually known as West Hill. In 1759 Penelope Pitt, a wealthy heiress and wife of George Pitt (later Lord Rivers), bought 41 acres south of West Hill from the Duke of Bedford. She built a small house, later described as 'an elegant cassino', where she gave parties and played at haymaking. The grounds were transformed by Capability Brown into parkland, with lakes and a home farm.

In 1789 the estate was bought by John Anthony Rucker. Rucker had been born in Hamburg in 1719, and was subsequently naturalised in England. He had formerly lived at Carshalton, where he was a partner of Francis Nixon, the calico-printer of Merton. He was also a merchant in partnership with various nephews and great-nephews, and the Ruckers continued to be prominent in Wandsworth life until the twentieth century. He was already 70 when he purchased the West Hill estate, but nevertheless proceeded to build the large house, designed by Jesse Gibson of Hackney, which still stands there. Rucker also enlarged the grounds, and employed Humphry Repton to improve them. On his death in 1804 the estate passed to his nephew Daniel, who changed the house's name to Melrose Hall, though it reverted to West Hill after 1824.

In 1824, probably because of financial difficulties, he sold the estate to George Granville Leveson-Gower, Marquess of Stafford, one of the richest men in England, with vast estates. Three years later the Marquess was able to add 117 acres to the estate from Earl Spencer's park, including woods and game cover, which made shooting parties possible. His eldest son George Granville, Duke of Sutherland, inherited West Hill in 1833, and he and his wife Harriet, a niece of Earl Spencer, occupied that and other houses. They lived a life of ever-increasing extravagance, with much entertaining and travelling, and also produced a family of four sons and seven daughters. Following further purchases, Sutherland owned most of South Field. The sale of the estate in 1842 may have been an attempt at retrenchment, but may also have been prompted the by growth of Wandsworth. It was bought by John Augustus Beaumont with the intention of developing it as a building estate.

In 1862 the house was rented to accommodate Sa'id Pasha, viceroy of Egypt, who was visiting an international exhibition. The Pasha arrived with a dozen officials and 80 slaves, but found it so remote and dull that he left after two nights, leaving behind his entourage.[18] Later in the same year it was purchased by the Royal Hospital.

68. The Clock House, on West Hill opposite Sutherland Grove, built in about the 1760s and seen here in 1887, shortly before demolition (watercolour by A.E. Coleman).

69. *An assembly at Penelope Pitt's West Hill villa in the early 1780s, when it was leased to Viscount Stormont.*

70. *West Hill in 1810, as rebuilt in about 1790 by John Anthony Rucker.*

Mayors of Garratt

Mock elections for the office of Mayor of Garratt in the eighteenth century attracted huge crowds to the tiny hamlet. Similar ceremonies took place elsewhere in the country, but none lasted so long, were so famous or had similar radical political overtones.

The first recorded election was in 1747. One account of its origins, written in 1754 by one of the leading Wandsworth Quakers, claimed that the first Mayor had been elected in about 1690 by some watermen who were 'spending a merry day at the Leather Bottle'. A later version, from 1781, is that the elections had begun about 30 years earlier as a result of successful local opposition to the illegal enclosure of common land, the leader of this opposition becoming known as the Mayor of Garratt. This corresponds reasonably well with the date of the first recorded election, but there is no evidence of such a campaign against enclosures. The fame of the elections was spread by Samuel Foote's farce, *The Mayor of Garret* (1764), and from 1768 candidates were often from London and its environs rather than just the Wandsworth area.

The candidates were always poor tradesmen, usually with a drink problem and sometimes with a physical deformity. The main qualification was a quick wit. They assumed such titles as Lord Twankum (a cobbler and gravedigger), Squire Blowmedown (a Wandsworth waterman) and Sir Trincalo Boreas (a fishmonger).

The candidates first walked or rode in procession from Southwark, and then paraded in Wandsworth, sometimes in carts shaped like boats. In 1781 there were 'scaffoldings and booths erected in Wandsworth at every open space; these were filled with spectators to the topmost rows, and boys climbed to the topmost poles, flags and colours were hung across the road, and the place was crowded by a dense population full of activity and noise'. They then rode in procession along Garratt Lane, accompanied by the Clerk, the Recorder and the Master of Horse, who in 1781 rode at the head of the 'Garratt Cavalry', a troop of 40 boys mounted on ponies. At the hustings, on Garratt Green, each candidate had to swear an oath, 'handed down to us by the grand Volgee, by order of the great Chin Kaw Chipo, first Emperor of the Moon'. The huge crowds, estimated in 1781 as 20,000 or more, blocked the streets for hours. Pub landlords donated funds to provide the candidates' lavish costumes, and were well-rewarded: on one occasion the pubs ran dry and only water was left,

71. *The Leather Bottle, first recorded in 1721, seen here in about 1890. The building probably dates from the second half of the eighteenth century.*

72.   *Houses in Garratt, north of the Leather Bottle, in about 1890. Weather-boarded houses were once common in the Wandle valley.*

73.   *The procession through Wandsworth High Street at the 1781 election, drawn by Valentine Green. Sir William and Lady Blaize are being drawn in a carriage shaped like a boat. The artist is looking from outside the Ram Inn towards the Spread Eagle.*

selling at 2d per glass. Elections normally coincided with actual parliamentary elections and, at first, two Mayors were elected each time.

From the 1760s the elections were associated with radical politics, and John Wilkes and his supporters wrote some of the candidates' addresses. The candidates invariably stressed their patriotism and loyalty to the King, while decrying economic hardships and the lack of liberty for the labouring classes.

In 1781 there were six candidates:

'About three o'clock the candidates proceeded with their several equipages towards the hustings; his Lordship [Lord Viscount Swallowtail, a basketmaker] was elegantly seated in a wicker cage, which was mounted on a cart and driven by a servant in a laced livery. The next in order was Sir John Harper [an inkle-weaver], who rode uncovered in a phaeton drawn by six horses, and was dressed in white and silver, with a blue ribband round his shoulder; this worthy knight recruited his spirits every furlong by a glass of Geneva ... After him came Sir T. Blaize [a blacksmith] mounted on a cart-horse, with a pack-saddle and halter, and paper ears reaching to the ground. Sir Christopher [a waterman] rode triumphantly in a boat drawn by four horses and filled with many emblematical devices.'

The press of carriages, waggons and horses prevented these candidates reaching the hustings, but Jeffrey Dunstan, 'proceeding without noise or ostentation', arrived at the Green on his own and proceeded to address the electors until interrupted by the hustings platform collapsing. 'The other candidates then not appearing, and a message being received from Sir John [Harper] that he was too drunk to attend, he was declared duly elected'.

Dunstan, the most celebrated of the Mayors, was a seller of second-hand wigs in the West End. He was a little over four feet tall, with knock-knees and a disproportionately large head. He had 'a countenance and manner marked by irresistible humour, and he never appeared without a train of boys and curious persons whom he entertained by his sallies of wit, shrewd sayings and smart repartees'. Dunstan remained Mayor until 1796 and was said to have died the following year as the result of a drinking spree.

Dunstan's successor was Henry Dinsdale (Sir Harry Dimsdale), described as 'a deformed dwarf, little better than an idiot, who used to cry muffins in the streets about St Anne's Soho'. He lived in

74. *Another drawing by Valentine Green in 1781: the carriage containing Sir John Harper (actually James Anderson, a breeches-maker and inkle-weaver) is passing the Leather Bottle.*

75. Jeffrey Dunstan, first elected as Mayor of Garratt in 1781.

76. Henry Dinsdale, elected Mayor of Garratt in 1796 and 1804.

a small attic near Seven Dials. In 1804, he stood as the Emperor Anti-Napoleon, addressing his subjects as the 'Emperor of Garratt'. However, the custom had been declining in popularity since the 1790s, as it became a symbol of plebeian mindlessness and lost both its patrician patronage and the support of political radicals who increasingly emphasised education and orderliness. There were no more elections after 1804, apart from an unsuccessful attempt to revive the custom in 1826. Dinsdale died in about 1810.

From Town to Suburb

Wandsworth's growth accelerated after 1851, and was most rapid in the three decades from 1881, when the population increased from about 28,000 to 92,000. New streets and houses spread over the fields until the last major areas available for development succumbed in the 1930s. With the new streets came new churches, shops, public buildings, factories, wharves, railways and a Thames bridge, as described in later chapters.

The first major development occurred in the west of the parish, and was untypical of what came later. John Augustus Beaumont purchased the West Hill estate in 1842 and Wimbledon Park in 1846. He laid out Inner Park Road, Princes Way, Beaumont Road, Augustus Road, Albert Drive and roads south of West Hill, dividing up the land for large villas for wealthy merchants and bankers. However, development was slow. By 1865, there was a continuous line of grand houses along

77. John Augustus Beaumont (1806-86), managing director of the County Fire Office and developer of Wimbledon Park.

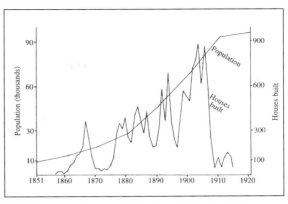

78. Wandsworth's population from 1851 to 1921 and the numbers of houses built each year. Numbers of houses are from building notices to 1870 and then from District Surveyors' returns. The figures to 1870 are less reliable because the houses for which permission was requested were not always built.

Park Side and much of West Hill, but only scattered development on the other roads; Princes Way, Albert Drive, Victoria Drive, Beaumont Road and Augustus Road were virtually untouched. Evidently the demand for large houses was limited, and smaller houses would not sell without better transport.

Another area of early development was south of Wandsworth Common. By 1865 there was a scattering of houses on the former Wandsworth Lodge estate, especially in Brodrick, Nottingham and Althorp Roads, even though the nearby Wandsworth Common Station did not open until 1869. The estate was developed by the British Land Company, which at first was as interested in creating freehold plots and therefore votes as in actual building.[1] Other relatively recent developments in 1865 were small houses in parts of Merton Road, the Ironmill Place area and the western part of Allfarthing Lane, and large ones in St Ann's Crescent.

The main developments of the later 1860s and 1870s were very large houses on the western edge of the parish in Keswick and Portinscale Roads, smaller houses in the area from Amerland Road to Lebanon Gardens developed by the British Land Company, the virtual completion of the street network in Bridge Field between East Hill and the railway and scattered developments elsewhere, particularly near St Anne's. Major developments in the 1880s included the area north of West Hill from Schubert Road to Santos Road (laid out in 1883), scattered streets elsewhere and much in Southfields and in Earlsfield north of the railway. Developments in the 1890s included the areas

79. *The centre of Wandsworth in 1865/6. The single most important change since has been the creation of Armoury Way, linking York Road and Putney Bridge Road via the north end of the Plain.*

80. *Allenswood, Albert Drive, one of the mansions built on Beaumont's estate, seen here in about 1904. It was a private girls' school from 1898 or earlier until the 1930s. Eleanor Roosevelt, later wife of US President F.D. Roosevelt, was a pupil there from 1898 to 1902.*

81. *Looking from the junction of West Hill and the Upper Richmond Road towards the Thames in about 1880, across the garden of Putney Lodge, on which Mexfield Road and other roads were about to be built.*

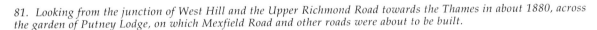

around Cicada Road (1891), Fawe Park Road (1893) and Rusholme Road (1894). By the end of the century the northern part of the parish was largely developed.

Building was financed in a variety of ways. For example, in 1868, Daniel Watney agreed with James Mason, a local builder, that Mason would build 33 houses in Ballantine Street (including a beershop), Watney advancing the money and, after each house was built and the loan was repaid, granting Mason a 99-year lease of the land.[2] More often, the landowner (sometimes a property company) laid out the street and sold plots or groups of plots to individual builders. Many builders were in fact craftsmen who sub-contracted much of the work once they agreed to build a house. In the part of Southfields known as the Grid, 44 builders were involved during the fourteen years of building, of whom the three largest built 43% of the houses and eighteen built fewer than ten houses each. Of those three largest builders, Ryan and Penfold were a builder and a solicitor (the latter an advocate of improvements in working-class housing), both of whom lived locally; Charles Barwell of Merton was from a family long active locally as builders; and George Gale was an estate agent, who acted as the link between the surveyor, Douglas Matthews of Fulham Road and the craftsmen who actually put up the houses. Develop-

ment was sometimes fast, notably in Trefoil Road, where all 54 houses were built in 1893-4, but sometimes much slower, an extreme case being Ringford Road, authorised in 1869 but the houses being built from 1877 to 1898.[3] The pace of development was often affected by the peaks and troughs of London's building cycle.

As the new suburbs grew, the perceived boundaries between parishes tended to blur and drift, especially in response to railway station names. Thus people in the western part of Wandsworth, such as the Attlees in Portinscale Road, regarded themselves as part of Putney, and the name East Putney has stuck to a large part of western Wandsworth. In the other direction, Wandsworth was considered more desirable than Battersea, so a new station opened in 1858 in Battersea Rise was named New Wandsworth, giving its name to a large part of western Battersea. In this case the station closed in 1869 and the name, though still current in 1902,[4] eventually disappeared. In the south-east of the parish, Thomas Hardy, living on the corner of Trinity and Brodrick Roads in 1878-81, dated his letters from Upper Tooting. The old parish boundaries lost much of their remaining significance when the London boroughs were created in 1900. The last perambulation of Wandsworth's boundary took place in 1898.[5]

82. Engadine Street, Southfields, part of the Grid, in about 1911.

SOUTHFIELDS

In Southfields the District Railway north of the station and Wimbledon Park Road to its south formed a sharp division between Beaumont's tree-lined streets and large villas to the west and the terraced houses to the east. Balvernie Grove and neighbouring streets, Standen Road and part of Penwith Road were laid out in the 1860s and 1870s. The District Railway opened in 1889, and the triangular area including Gartmoor and Southdean Gardens was laid out in the same year. Approval for the roads comprising the Grid, between Replingham and Revelstoke Roads, was obtained by the Wimbledon Park Land Company Ltd in three stages: southwards to Brookwood Road in 1891, to Lavenham Road in 1899 and to Revelstoke Road in 1903. Strathville Street and neighbouring streets were authorised in 1901 and Pulborough Road and roads leading off it in 1907.

The example of the Grid shows that the demand for new housing in Southfields at first remained low, even after the railway opened, for areas with better transport links were still available elsewhere. By 1894, of the north-south streets authorised, only Elsenham and Heythorp Streets had been laid out and only eleven houses had been built in them; Trentham and Elborough Streets still had no houses in 1898. Development accelerated in 1899, and the small-scale building of the 1890s gave way to

84. Augustus Road in the late nineteenth century, indicating how rural much of the former Wimbledon Park remained.

construction of houses in blocks of fifty or so. The last of the Grid's 1757 houses and shops were completed by the end of 1907. For long afterwards there was still much open land west of the District Railway, including Skinners Wood west of the station, which did not succumb until 1929.

Not much survived from the earlier landscape. The mid-eighteenth-century carriageway from Tibbet's Corner to the Spencers' house became Victoria Drive, the older Green Street (alias the Great Baulk, a baulk being the headland between

83. Magdalen Road, seen from Garratt Lane in about 1900. The Baptist church on the right was built in 1898.

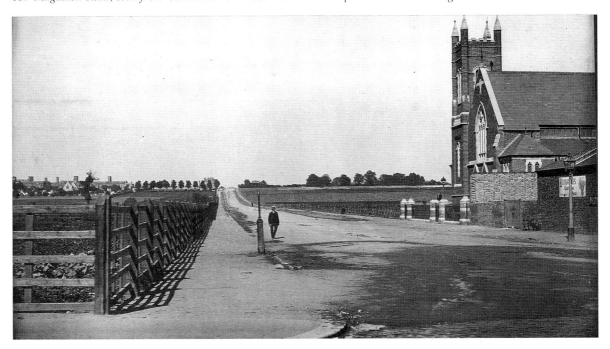

two open field shots) is now Granville Road, a footpath west of Merton Road called The Baulk marks another headland, and Wimbledon Park Road follows the line of the ancient track from Wandsworth to Wimbledon.

EARLSFIELD

The key figure in Earlsfield's early development was Robert Davis, who bought Elm Lodge, Allfarthing Lane, in 1868 and added a new house there called Earlsfield, a reference to his wife's maiden name of Earl. He obtained a further 59 acres in 1876 and began building shortly afterwards. Earlsfield Road was authorised in 1878, and gave its name to the railway station and the whole area.[6] Neither Garratt nor Summerstown, being poor areas, acted as nuclei from which building spread.

The opening of Earlsfield Station in 1884 greatly stimulated development. The British Land Company purchased the lower part of Davis's estate in 1885, and much of the area in the angle of Garratt Lane and Earlsfield Road, as far as Swaffield Road and Westover Road, was laid out between 1885 and 1888. Summerly, Skelbrook and Trewint Streets were authorised in 1882, as were Baskerville Road and the other roads forming the so-called toast-rack. The other streets between Allfarthing

Lane and Earlsfield Road were authorised in 1891 and 1897.

By 1900, Earlsfield north of the railway was fully built up, but there were hardly any buildings south of the railway, except in the toast-rack area. Magdalen Road had been laid out in the late 1870s and named after Magdalen College, Oxford, which then owned much of southern Earlsfield, but it did not become built-up until the following century, and at first served only the cemetery. The segment from Garratt Lane to Swaby Road was laid out between 1900 and 1906, and the area between Loxley Road and Magdalen Road in the same years, and development then gradually proceeded until the area from Fieldview to Tilehurst Road was built over in 1933/4.

VICTORIAN INHABITANTS

We can explore the new suburb using the 1891 census and Charles Booth's map of 1898-9 allocating the streets among seven categories according to the wealth or poverty of their inhabitants, though Booth's map unfortunately covers only the northern part of the parish. The general pattern was that the poorer areas were between the Thames and the railway and along the Wandle valley, together with the Iron Mill Place area west of St Ann's Hill. In the eastern part of the former parish

85. Earlsfield Road in about 1919.

Mansion·at·Wandsworth·Common
now·in·course·of·erection
E·R·ROBSON ARCHT·

86. *A mansion at Wandsworth Common 'now in course of erection' in June 1876 – the sort of house which fell into Booth's 'wealthy' category.*

south of the railway there were several streets of 'poverty & comfort (mixed)' near the railway, but otherwise all were 'fairly comfortable' or occasionally 'well-to-do'. West of the Wandle valley, the range was from 'fairly comfortable' to Booth's highest class, 'wealthy'.

The 'wealthy' areas included most of West Hill, the Upper Richmond Road, Keswick and Portinscale Roads and, to the east, Spencer Park. Portinscale Road, for example, was occupied in 1891 by two merchants, two solicitors, a submarine engineer, a builder, a Chancery registrar, an Assistant Secretary at the Board of Trade, a gardener, a retired tea merchant and a man with private means. They averaged between three and four servants each.

Booth's 'well-to-do' areas were scattered, though they included most of the area around Melrose Road. Cromford Road provides an example. Clerks were the most numerous occupational group there in 1891: together with the managers of businesses, commercial travellers, engineers and other professionals (a draughtsman, an architect, a financial

journalist, an optician and so on) they accounted for almost two-thirds of the houses; many other inhabitants were retired or had private means. Almost all had one servant. This was a typical commuter street.

Streets categorised as a mixture of 'fairly comfortable' and 'well-to-do' included most of those south and east of St Anne's Church. 'Fairly comfortable' applied to almost the whole area between East Hill and the railway to Richmond. Servants were almost unknown in these streets. In Dempster Road, one of the 'fairly comfortable' streets, there was a great mixture of occupations, such as clerks, building workers, designers, a gunmaker, a railway ticket collector, a government telegraphist and a judge's attendant.

Streets of mixed poverty and comfort included Palmerston and Coliston Roads (off Merton Road), most of the roads on the east side of Garratt Lane from Allfarthing Lane to the High Street and roads near Wandsworth Station on either side of York Road. In Sudlow Road, north of Frogmore, with six rooms per house, labourers, building workers and transport workers accounted for almost two-thirds of the households in 1891.

Areas of 'moderate poverty' included Point Pleasant, most of the alleys around the High Street and Frogmore, Iron Mill Place, Warple Road, Eltringham Street and Jews Row. Typical inhabitants in all of these were labourers, building workers, transport workers and industrial workers – two-thirds of the total in both Point Pleasant and Warple Road. At Apothecaries Row, in Warple Road, the houses consisted of cellar, sitting room, bedroom and attic.[7] A rare survival of one of Booth's areas of moderate poverty is Prospect Cottages, Point Pleasant.

As for Booth's two worst categories, 'very poor' was almost unrepresented, but Hills Yard, on the west side of the Plain, was ascribed to the 'lowest class'. According to Booth, this reflected 'the presence of low-class prostitutes'.

However, Booth also believed poverty and slums were spreading along the Wandle valley, and he described Wardley Street and Lydden Grove as the worst of those streets, summarising the former as follows:

'Houses two-storeyed, most of them flush with the pavement; a low common lodging-house on one side and a yard full of wheelless gipsy vans on the other, each inhabited by a family. There is throughout the street a family to almost every room, and a great number of loafers hang about at the corner – men who work either not at all, or only on market days.'

This called forth an angry and detailed response from the local Medical Officer. The 78 houses included two lodging houses and nine houses let as lodgings, but only 25 families occupied a single room and these were nearly always a man and his wife without children; 25 families had four or more rooms. The occupations of the males were: hawkers and costers 64, general labourers 32, carmen 9, bricklayers 3, plasterers 2, Council employees 3 – 'the rest consist of tinkers, wood choppers and rag and bone dealers'. There was also a yard occupied by costers and their vans. His explanation for the number of costers was that their vans were cleared from the Common at the time Wardley Street was built. The sanitary arrangements were satisfactory, but insanitary con-

87. Wardley Street, west of Garratt Lane, authorised in 1867 and seen here in 1956, shortly before demolition.

88. *F. Kent, fishmonger, on the corner of Hills Yard (to the left) and the Plain in 1886.*

ditions sometimes resulted from careless habits ('The people themselves seem to have an instinctive dislike to soap and water'). There was little poverty, and rents were generally paid regularly.[8] Much of course depended on how one defined poverty, insanitary conditions and slums. Lindsay Glegg, who first visited Wardley Street in 1905, later described it as 'one of the worst slums in London', where policemen always patrolled in pairs.[9]

Booth mentioned 'two colonies of gipsies, costers, flower sellers, and the like. In Summer the gipsies go to fairs, and before the start for Epsom in the Derby week the place is a pandemonium. The houses are many of them owned by the richer members of the clan; and room is found for vans, with wheels or without, in which the poorer members crowd'. Wardley Street was evidently one of these.

NOTABLE INHABITANTS

Jenny Lind (1820-87), the most famous singer of her day and known as 'the Swedish nightingale', moved to Argyle Lodge, Park Side, in 1859. In 1863 she bought land in Victoria Drive (where Weydown and Smithwood Closes now stand) and there built Oaklea, named after the trees in the garden. She often invited the choir of Holy Trinity, West Hill, to Oaklea for an evening's music. In 1874 she decided she needed to be nearer central London, and moved to South Kensington.[10]

Mary Ann Evans, better-known as the novelist, George Eliot (1819-80), moved to Holly Lodge, Wimbledon Park Road (now No. 31) with her lover, George Henry Lewes, in February 1859. She was soon enthusing about 'glorious breezy walks, and wide horizons, well ventilated rooms, and abundant water'. Their domestic routine was work in the morning, lunch at 1.30, an afternoon

89. *W. Prior, hairdresser etc., 52 Wandsworth High Street (just west of the town hall). He traded there from about 1902 to 1915.*

90. *Bird & Sons, 461 Garratt Lane (on the east side north of Algarve Road). They traded there from about 1908 until the 1920s, and then at 557 Garratt Lane until the 1940s.*

91. *E.J. Seaton, bootmaker and repairer at 31 Barmouth Road from about 1901 to 1920.*

walk and dinner at 6.30 followed by reading aloud or music. *The Mill on the Floss* was written at Holly Lodge. It was soon after moving there that her identity became known, resulting in visits from other literary figures such as Dickens.

However, she soon became disillusioned with Southfields, apparently because of the lack of seclusion and space and the remoteness from a railway station – 'it is a fatiguing ugly walk to Wandsworth Station – we always go to Putney when we can'. In late 1859 she wrote that 'I should like to transfer our present house, into which we were driven by haste and economy, to someone who likes houses full of eyes round him. I long for a house with some shade and grass close round it'. In September they moved to Regents Park.[11]

Thomas Hardy (1840-1928) took a three-year lease of The Larches, Trinity Road (now No. 172) in February 1878, having decided that his profession of novelist required him to live near London. Here he wrote *A Laodicean*. By 1881 he had decided that a country residence was better both for his health and inspiration, residence near a city having 'tended to force mechanical and ordinary

productions from his pen', and he moved to Wimborne.[12]

Another writer, H.G. Wells (1866-1946), moved in 1891 to 28 Haldon Road with his aunt and his cousin, Isabel Mary Wells, whom he married at All Saints Church later in the year. Wells was then 25 and a journalist. In 1893 the Wells moved to Sutton, and shortly afterwards the couple separated. His first novel, *The Time Machine*, was published two years later.[13]

Charles Pearson (1793-1862), who moved to Wandsworth in about 1852, was more than anyone else responsible for the building of the world's first underground railway, the Metropolitan from Paddington to Farringdon Street. He was a solicitor and a supporter of radical causes, including cheap travel for artisans. In 1846 he proposed a central railway station for the City at Farringdon Street, and this eventually developed into a plan for a railway under Euston Road. Pearson died in 1862 at his home, Oxford Lodge, West Hill Road, a few months before the Metropolitan Railway opened.[14]

David Lloyd George (1863-1945) moved to 193 Trinity Road in November 1899, while still a backbencher. In about 1904 he transferred to 3 Routh Road, retaining it until 1907, by which time he was a Cabinet Minister. On Saturday mornings he could often be seen at Wandsworth Common

92. Jenny Lind.

93. George Eliot.

94. *David Lloyd George in about 1909.*

95. *George Dixon Longstaff in about 1880.*

Station with his golf clubs over his shoulder. His wife regarded their period in Wandsworth as 'a very happy time ... without any responsibility'.[15]

Clement Attlee (1883-1967) was born at Westcott, 18 Portinscale Road. His grandfather had been a miller at Dorking and his father was a solicitor; his mother's family lived at The Gables on North Side. Clement was the seventh of eight children. The 1891 census records Ellen Attlee (her husband being absent), five children including Clement, a cook, a nurse, a parlourmaid and a housemaid. Clement Attlee's childhood was a happy one. On Sunday mornings his father would 'take us for walks before church round the market gardens which then lay between Putney and Wandsworth'. After periods at school and university Clement was living in Portinscale Road when he began helping at the boys' club in Stepney, which was the decisive event in forming his political beliefs. In 1920 his mother died and the house in Portinscale Road was sold.[16]

An important figure locally was George Dixon Longstaff (1799-1892). He was born in Bishopwearmouth, County Durham, to a family of distinguished engineers (his brother helped make the railway locomotive *Sanspareil* for the Rainhill trials in 1829). He qualified as a doctor in 1828, and was the first teacher of practical chemistry to medical students. He practised as a physician in Hull, spent some years in North Carolina applying his scientific knowledge to gold mining, and, having married Maria Blundell, worked with his father-in-law as a manufacturer of oil, colours and varnish, becoming for many years chairman of Blundell, Spence & Co. This brought him in 1837 to Wandsworth, where the firm had a candle factory by the Wandle just south of the former Adkins Mill and where he lived for the rest of his life. He was one of the founders of the Chemical Society of London and the Society of Chemical Industry and was active in the promotion of Mechanics' Institutes. From 1855 he lived at Butterknowle in Melrose Road. He was a vestryman, one of the first members of the Wandsworth District Board of Works and active in many other local organisations, and he also provided the Longstaff Reading Room which still forms part of West Hill Library. He died at Butterknowle in 1892, aged 92.[17]

96. *The coach yard at the Spread Eagle, drawn by George Scharf on 16 July 1839. Scharf is looking south from the main part of the inn in the High Street; the Assembly Room is on the right.*

On the Move

Before the railways, transport to and from Wandsworth was by road or river. The early turnpiking, in 1718, of the road from London to Kingston and Portsmouth via Wandsworth High Street and West Hill indicates its importance, and probably resulted in increased use of the roads in preference to the river. From the 1650s there were stage coaches through Wandsworth, and by the late eighteenth century Wandsworth had its own stage coaches to and from London. In 1793 there were three separate firms, each with a morning and an afternoon or early evening departure daily. By 1838 there were also omnibuses, a larger vehicle providing a cheaper service. Robert Barchard stated in 1845 that Wandsworth to London Bridge took three-quarters of an hour by omnibus and not more than half an hour by horse and gig. By the 1840s there were steamboats calling at the pier opposite the Ship pub.[1]

THE RICHMOND RAILWAY

The London and Southampton Railway (later the London & South Western Railway, or LSWR) opened through Wandsworth parish in 1838. The first station out of Nine Elms (then the London terminus) was known as Wandsworth, and later as Clapham Common, but was in fact in Battersea parish. It was on the north side of Battersea Rise bridge, and attracted few passengers – not surprisingly, since the journey from Wandsworth to London, involving a cab or a boat from Nine Elms, took an hour;[2] it was replaced in 1863 by Clapham Junction.

In 1845 the Richmond Railway Company began to build a line from Falcon Bridge (now Clapham Junction) to Richmond. The LSWR was to operate the line, and also to extend its own line from Nine Elms to Waterloo. Bridge and steamboat owners had opposed the line, while Wandsworth Vestry was neutral. The railway opened in July 1846, ahead of time and at less than the estimated cost – both unusual occurrences. The viaduct over the Wandle valley and the cutting towards Putney were the only substantial engineering works involved. Unlike the London and Southampton line it was mainly intended for commuter and excursion traffic rather than goods traffic.

97. *The Richmond Railway's Wandle viaduct, drawn in 1846. The larger arch on the left crossed the Cut; that on the right crossed the Wandle. The viaduct still carries trains, but has been widened with an extra track on each side.*

Wandsworth Station was at first on the east side of Fairfield Street. It was relocated to its present position in about 1860, for reasons unknown. The new station was rebuilt in 1886 when the line was doubled to four tracks, and the building of 1886 was in turn demolished in 1988 when the station was refurbished. It was renamed Wandsworth Town in 1903.

When the Richmond line opened there were seventeen trains a day from Wandsworth. They were approximately hourly from 8.11am, and only four carried third-class passengers. Such a service was useless for the working classes, who could not usually afford to live far from their work anyway, but it was probably helpful to wealthier commuters. In fact it had little immediate impact, Wandsworth being only one of many parishes now more accessible to London. Nevertheless, it created the potential for suburban growth, and the service on the line eventually increased consider-

98. *Earlsfield Station, seen from the corner of Magdalen Road in about 1911.*

ably. The Vicar of All Saints noted in 1902 that 'Large numbers go by train to their work; thirteen hundred before eight o'clock in the morning, by the workmen's trains; the clerks between eight and nine; and the few privileged ones an hour later. All return between six and nine in the evening'.[3] The line was electrified in 1915-16.

At first the railways made little effort to attract short-distance traffic, and after 1863 there was no station between Clapham Junction and Wimbledon until 1884, when Earlsfield (originally Earlsfield and Summerstown) was opened. It was built following a campaign by the Vicar of St Mary's Summerstown, estate agents, builders and others to make the area more attractive to commuters. Local agitation for a station in the Heathfield Road area in 1889[4] and an LSWR plan for the same in 1916 came to nothing. Wandsworth Common Station, just inside Battersea parish, opened in 1869.

WANDSWORTH BRIDGE

The first Wandsworth Bridge was authorised by an Act of 1864, and was built by a private company with the intention of making a profit through tolls. In 1865 the company expected the bridge to become a means of access to the proposed terminus of the Hammersmith and City Railway on its north side, though this was never built. Following prolonged financial and contractual difficulties, the bridge was opened in 1873. In 1880 the Metropolitan Board of Works bought out the proprietors and freed the bridge from tolls. The bridge was poorly-constructed, too weak for heavy traffic, too narrow and had awkward approaches. In the 1890s it was thought to have less traffic than any other Thames bridge in London.[5]

There were demands for the bridge's rebuilding and the improvement of its southern approach from 1912, and the present bridge, designed in 1936, was opened to traffic in 1940. Many schemes later a new southern approach linking the bridge to Trinity Road was eventually opened in 1969.[6]

TRAMS

Horse-trams reached Wandsworth in the 1880s. Twice as many passengers could be hauled per horse in a tram as in an omnibus, so the trams were much cheaper. The South London Tramways Company was authorised to build two lines terminating in Wandsworth and linking it with (initially) Vauxhall and Southwark Bridge (they were not allowed into central London). The 'top road' began on East Hill by the present Book House. The 'lower road' was from the south end of Fairfield Street along Fairfield Street and York Road. Both were single track with passing places, and they opened in 1882 and 1883 respectively. The company also built a depot at Jews Row, with stabling for 1200 horses.[7]

The Wandsworth District Board of Works was at best lukewarm and at worst obstructive towards trams, apparently because of the effect of tram noise on property values, but others saw them as a way of providing cheap transport which enabled the working classes to live in less crowded areas

99. *The first Wandsworth Bridge, drawn in 1874. It was a cut-price design by Julian Tolmé, and was opened in 1873.*

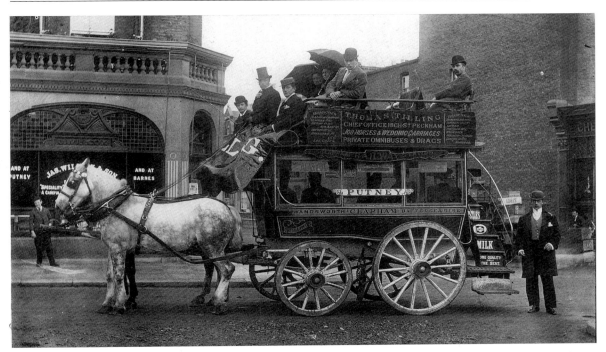

100. *A horse-bus at the junction of West Hill and the Upper Richmond Road (at the corner of Mexfield Road) in the 1890s.*

101. *A horse-tram in Fairfield Street, near the terminus, in about 1905.*

102. Heavy traffic in the High Street in about 1900.

further from their work. London County Council acquired the South London lines in 1902 and immediately set about electrifying and extending them. York Road, which hitherto ended at Fairfield Street, was cut through to meet Ram Street in 1906, and electric trams then followed that route and continued along Garratt Lane to Tooting Broadway. Meanwhile, motor buses had begun operating through Wandsworth in 1905.[8] The trams' 'top road' was electrified in 1909. In 1912 the West London system through Hammersmith and Putney was extended along Putney Bridge Road to its junction with the High Street, but not until the High Street had been widened could that tramway be extended to meet the 'lower road' and the 'top road' (in 1915 and 1921 respectively).

The Wandsworth, Tooting and Putney lines were converted to trolleybus operation in 1937, although some trams remained along York Road until 1950. The trolleybuses were themselves superseded by motor buses in 1960. Petrol-engined vehicles have

of course transformed both transport and the environment in Wandsworth in the second half of the twentieth century.

THE METROPOLITAN DISTRICT RAILWAY

Wandsworth's third and last railway was the Metropolitan District Railway (now the District Line). Having spent heavily on its central London track the company was anxious to tap the developing suburban traffic to the south-west, in territory the LSWR regarded as its own. The District reached Putney Bridge Station in 1880, and in 1881 was authorised to build a line via East Putney Station across or under Putney Heath to Kingston and Surbiton. An independent scheme, authorised in 1882, was for a line connecting Putney Bridge Station and the LSWR main line at Wimbledon. The latter was strongly backed by J.A. Beaumont, who believed the new line would

103. *Electrifying the tram route in York Road in 1906.*

104. *Trams in Wandsworth Garage in 1950. The garage had been virtually rebuilt to house electric trams in 1906. It remains in use for buses.*

105. *Southfields Station, opened in 1889, seen here in about 1908.*

promote the development of Wimbledon Park and double its value; indeed one opponent said that the Bill 'might almost be called a Beaumont Estate bill and not a railway bill'.

In the event both sets of promoters failed to raise enough money, and their powers were passed to the LSWR, which abandoned the Kingston route but built the Wimbledon line. When the line opened in 1889, both the LSWR and the District used it (the LSWR gaining access from connecting lines east of Putney Station), but the District provided three-quarters of the trains.

Services on the new railway and housing development increased hand in hand. In 1905 the line was electrified, and by 1914 there were 108 trains a day to Mansion House, more than three times as many as in 1891, including 24 arriving before 9am. LSWR services from Wimbledon to Waterloo via East Putney were always less frequent, and they ceased in 1941.

GOODS TRANSPORT

Water carriage was mostly organised from the channels around the Wandle mouth, together with the Surrey Iron Railway's dock (later known as the Cut), although there were also several wharves on the Thames and a landing place by the

Waterman's Arms. Hogmore, which had formerly provided access to the Wandle and thus to the Thames, was leased by the lord of Battersea and Wandsworth Manor to Hugh Cumlyn in 1733, and although legal action in 1753 to maintain public access appears to have been successful, public access was eventually lost.[9] Between 1838 and 1866 an arm of the Wandle just east of the present Sudlow Road was converted into a small dock.

From 1805 coal and other commodities could be brought direct from the north and Midlands to Wandsworth via the Grand Junction Canal, Brentford Dock and the Thames. In 1811, Anthony Lyon, later recorded as a barge-builder and lighterman at Railway Wharf on the Cut, had 50 lighters, each able to carry 60 tons. After the Surrey Iron Railway closed the Cut was owned successively by Messrs Watney and Wells, millers, and William McMurray, papermaker, and was sometimes known as McMurray's Canal. In 1866 McMurray fought off a plan to use it as part of a canal to Wimbledon. In 1932-7, the gas company, which had acquired the Cut and needed the land, filled it in. The small dock east of Sudlow Road and the arm towards Frogmore seem to have been filled in in about 1960, but Bell Lane Creek, proposed for filling in in 1958, remains.[10]

106. *Aerial view of about 1925, showing, from left to right, the Cut, the Wandle, the Causeway, Bell Lane Creek and the small dock. Railway Wharf was to the left of the Cut. The Plain is near the top on the right.*

The railways provided goods facilities at New Wandsworth Station (on the south side of Battersea Rise), and Wandsworth Common Station, opened in 1858 and 1869 respectively, and there were later sidings at Point Pleasant; all these closed in the 1960s. There was also the option of road transport. In 1866 Henry Knight, papermaker at Garratt Mill, obtained heavy goods from London either by water or by rail to New Wandsworth, but sent out his paper by cart, which saved having to tranship it twice before final delivery in London.[11]

107. *A busy scene on the Wandle in about 1905, apparently in the dock just east of Sudlow Road.*

Civic Life

VESTRY AND BOARD OF WORKS

Until 1856, Wandsworth continued to be governed by the parish Vestry, though it lost its responsibility for policing in 1830 and for administering the Poor Law in 1834. However, the amateur status of its officials and insufficient powers made it an increasingly inadequate form of government for a developing urban area. When London's local government was reformed in 1856, Wandsworth joined Battersea, Clapham, Streatham, Tooting Graveney and Putney in the Wandsworth District Board of Works. The Board had several full-time officials, as well as part-time medical officers for each parish. Committees were set up for each of the six parishes, though Putney and Wandsworth were combined. The District Board created a great deal that is now taken for granted, including the local sewers, wider roads, kerbs and pavements, and it also made effective use of its powers to fight contagious diseases such as cholera. When Battersea parish exercised its right to opt out of the District Board in 1887, the Board needed to move from its offices from Battersea Rise, and erected what is now Book House on East Hill.[1]

109. *Wandsworth Town Hall, designed by George Patrick and built with red brick and Dumfries stone in French Renaissance style in 1881, on the north side of the High Street opposite the Friends' Meeting House. On the ground floor were parish offices and a small hall used for Vestry meetings and upstairs was a public hall seating 600.*

108. *Wandsworth District Board of Works' offices, erected in 1887-8 to the design of W. Newton Dunn at the junction of East Hill and North Side. It is now Book House, headquarters of the Book Trust.*

110. *Celebrating Queen Victoria's diamond jubilee in 1897. The platform has been erected around the drinking fountain at the junction of Garratt Lane (to the right) and the High Street.*

The vestries remained in existence, becoming 'closed' bodies again, elected by the ratepayers and themselves electing the members of the District Board. They retained substantial powers, and it was Wandsworth Vestry which established the first library and swimming baths. It also erected a new town hall in 1881.

Wandsworth became a parliamentary constituency in 1885, though it covered more than just Wandsworth. London County Council was created in 1889, its main impact locally being on tramways and open spaces and later on housing. The next major change was the replacement of the District Board by the Borough of Wandsworth in 1900, covering the same area. (The only subsequent change has been the removal of Clapham and Streatham and the addition of Battersea in 1965.) Civic pride in Wandsworth was probably at its peak in about 1900, and several amenities were created at that time, including parks, libraries and the swimming baths, in a few cases by donation from wealthy inhabitants. Wandsworth's local newspaper started as a Putney venture in 1884, became the *Putney and Wandsworth Borough News* in 1885 and later dropped the words *Putney and*.[2]

WATER, SEWERS AND PUBLIC HEALTH

In 1852 parts of Wandsworth obtained a supply of piped water, provided by the Southwark and Vauxhall Water Company, but it was taken from the Thames and was inadequately filtered and famously impure, as well as insufficient in quantity. Most inhabitants then obtained their water from wells or from the Wandle. Wells were increasingly unsatisfactory, because of seepage from cesspools, although there was a deep well at Young's Brewery from which many people obtained water. Wandle water was taken chiefly from a place left open for the purpose beside the Wandle bridge, from which water carriers fetched it to sell by the pailful. It was regarded as far superior to Thames water, though that was not saying much. A local property-owner noted in 1852 that 'from the impurities which are thrown into the Wandle, sometimes it does not look very tempting; at other times it is very pure'.[3] However, in 1858 the local Medical Officer referred to 'the revolting fact that great numbers of the poorer classes are still compelled to drink the water of the Thames and Wandle, which is but sewage more or less diluted'. Some of the houses towards the north end of Garratt Lane had privies over-

111. Outside Wandsworth Town Hall at the General Election of 1906.

hanging the very river from which they obtained
their water. The quality of the Wandle water
undoubtedly declined as the population along its
course increased. Between 70 and 80 people died
of cholera in Wandsworth in 1854.[4]

Wandsworth increasingly depended on piped
water, but in the 1870s and early 1880s its Medical
Officer was still complaining of the impurity of
Southwark and Vauxhall water (still taken from
the tidal Thames and noted in 1871 as containing
'moving organisms visible to the naked eye') and
the absence of a constant supply, which meant
water having to be stored in cisterns. By 1885 the
water was reckoned sufficiently pure if drunk
from the mains, but there was still no constant
supply.

The other great necessity – sewers – began to
be supplied in a small way by the parish in 1849,
following a cholera outbreak,[5] but in 1857 the
Medical Officer noted 'the disgusting open cesspools which abound throughout the parish'. Not
until the 1860s, when the Metropolitan Board of

Works completed the main low-level and high-
level sewers and the District Board built the local
network was the problem addressed.

In 1860 the Medical Officer noted the dispropor-
tionate mortality among the labouring classes,
particularly the children, and emphasised the need
for effective water supply, drainage and rubbish
removal, especially in courts and alleys. He
continued to make similar points for many years,
though public health did gradually improve.

POLICE AND FIRE SERVICES

Until 1830 order was kept in Wandsworth by the
parish constable. The watchhouse was east of the
Wandle bridge until 1753, then east of the churchyard and from 1820 on the west side of the Plain
at the north end.[6] The Metropolitan Police Force
was established in 1829, and in the following year
its Wandsworth Division was created, extending
to South Lambeth, Tooting, Putney, Barnes and
Fulham. The police station in Putney Bridge Road

112. *The aqueduct, built in 1882-5 to carry the southern high-level sewer across the Wandle valley and demolished in 1968. This view, of about 1907 (before the creation of King George's Park) is looking east from Merton Road. The larger arch was where the aqueduct crossed Buckhold Road.*

was established in the 1830s, and was replaced by the present police station on West Hill in 1883. Earlsfield Police Station in Garratt Lane opened in 1914.[7]

Wandsworth's police station included a magistrates' court from 1839, but the courtroom was very cramped – only twenty feet by sixteen. After decades of complaints, a new court was eventually provided in Battersea in 1892. The county court was being held in the Spread Eagle assembly room by 1857, but from 1860 until 1973 it used the purpose-built courthouse a few yards away (now Wandsworth Museum).[8]

The parish had long taken some responsibility for tackling fires. In 1752 money was subscribed for two fire engines and an engine house, which was built on the west side of the Plain and continued in use until the 1860s. The present site on West Hill has been used since 1892, although the building now there dates only from 1955.[9]

LIBRARIES

Wandsworth had some public library provision from an early date: in 1833 not only did the parish schools have lending libraries, but 'that at the National School is extended to the use of the poor of the parish generally'. Subsequently Wandsworth became only the second parish in London (after St Margaret and St John Westminster) to use the powers made available in 1850 to provide a public library. Wandsworth Library Commissioners were appointed in 1883 and the library

opened in 1885 in a large private house (Putney Lodge) on West Hill. Use of the library was far beyond expectations, and a reading room was added in 1887, the gift of Dr G.D. Longstaff.[10]

Books were not then on open shelves: readers consulted a printed catalogue and obtained books from the staff by quoting the catalogue number.

113. *Wandsworth police station from the 1830s until 1883, situated where Armoury Way now meets Putney Bridge Road.*

114. *The parish watch house and engine house on the west side of the Plain. The engine house served as a mortuary during the cholera outbreak of 1866.*

115. *Wandsworth's firemen outside the new fire station on West Hill opened in 1892.*

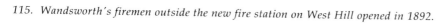

116. *West Hill Library (formerly Putney Lodge) with the Longstaff Reading Room in about 1905.*

117. *The Longstaff Reading Room in West Hill Library in about 1905. The room was retained when the rest of the library was rebuilt in 1937.*

118. The Huguenot Cemetery. In the background, facing North Side, is a red-brick house of the seventeenth or eighteenth century.

The first librarian was Alfred Cotgreave, who had invented the Cotgreave Indicator, a huge contraption which showed whether a book was 'in' or 'out'. The second librarian, Cecil Tudor Davis, was a keen local historian and wrote extensively. West Hill Library did not open its lending library shelves until 1937, following the building of a new library in that year.

Branch libraries were added in Allfarthing Lane in 1898, Earlsfield in 1926 and Southfields in 1934. Earlsfield Library retains its original building, but that of Southfields dates from 1956 (extensively rebuilt in 1990) and the Alvering Library in Allfarthing Lane from 1961.[11] In the 1950s Wandsworth's library network became the first in the country to issue books by a photographic method using microfilm cameras.

CEMETERIES

Wandsworth's cemeteries have constantly needed extension to cope with the growth in population. A new graveyard now known as the Huguenot Cemetery was acquired on former common land on East Hill in 1680. This coincided with the arrival of the Huguenots, and it became known in the early eighteenth century as the French Churchyard, though by no means all those buried there were Huguenots. Its other name, by the mid-eighteenth century, was Mount Nod, probably indicating that it was a place of sleep. It was extended westwards in 1735.[12] It narrowly escaped destruction in the 1960s for a slip road from Trinity Road. The Quakers had their own small burial ground from the seventeenth century, and ashes are still interred there.

The parish later opened another cemetery in Garratt Lane, consecrated in 1808. In 1853, under new public health legislation, burials at All Saints and Mount Nod ceased and those in the Garratt Lane ground were confined to one per grave. Wandsworth Cemetery in Magdalen Road was opened in 1878 and was later extended.[13]

119. All Saints Church as rebuilt in 1779. In the foreground are the stocks, and in the background is the house with Dutch gables.

Churches and Chapels

ALL SAINTS

Until the mid-seventeenth century all Wandsworth's inhabitants, apart from an occasional Catholic after the Reformation, were regular attenders at the parish church of All Saints. The churchwardens' accounts record the attempts to accommodate the growing population, including the addition of galleries – the first in 1597, a second by 1618 and a third in about 1647. The present tower, now the oldest building in the parish, was erected in 1630. Between 1716 and 1724 Mr Edgley, Vicar of Wandsworth for 44 years, added the present north aisle at his own cost in return for receiving the income from pews and burials in that part of the church.[1]

The church was largely rebuilt in 1779, though Edgley's north aisle and the tower were retained. The tower was refaced and raised in 1841, but the upper part was destroyed by bombing in 1941. In 1899-1900 the present chancel was added and the church was re-roofed.[2]

QUAKERS AND FRENCH PROTESTANTS

The Quakers erected their first meeting-house in Wandsworth in 1673, on the present site in the High Street. They were typically craftsmen or watermen, often from nearby villages. George Fox visited the meeting in 1680 and recorded that 'I had a very precious time with friends at Wandsworth'. They were constantly in trouble for not

120. Inside the Quakers' meeting-house in about 1900.

121. *The interior of the former French Chapel in 1832, when it was being used by an Independent congregation (watercolour by Edward Hassell).*

122. *The French Chapel, built or converted from an earlier building in the 1680s. It was south of the High Street, where the Memorial Hall is now. The inscription stating that it had been erected in 1573 was a later fabrication. The Presbyterians of the 1570s would not have advertised their existence by meeting in a purpose-built chapel, and the Dutch, sometimes suggested as early users of the building, were too few to have had their own chapel.*

attending the parish church and refusing to pay tithes. In 1681 Justice Foster entered the meeting-house 'as the Assembly was sitting in silence. The Justice scoffingly said, The Spirit does not move them. He then demanded their names, but they not answering, he asked their names of some that stood by, but they replied, They would not be informers. Whereupon he sent for the constable of the town, and he appearing unwilling to concern himself, the Justice threatned to fine him', following which he gave the names. The Quakers can hardly have been popular, but there seems to have been an unwillingness locally to persecute them; no-one would buy the boat seized on this occasion. In 1725 there were between 200 and 300 Quakers (probably not all resident in Wandsworth). The present meeting-house was built in 1778, and was given a new facade in 1927.[3]

The French Protestants were not dissenters from the Church of England; they simply used the Book of Common Prayer in a different language. The first Minister at Wandsworth, Elie Brevet, was given permission to leave his church in France in early 1682, and the Wandsworth Huguenots received a grant of £20 towards fitting a place for worship in July 1682. Their chapel was probably converted from an existing building: their appeal for funds in 1686 states that they 'did hire a place, by the price of five pounds a yeare, and desired a carpenter to undertake the work to make the said place fitt', costing somewhat over £140.[4]

The French Chapel's congregation gradually dwindled in the eighteenth century, and in 1787 the services were transferred to London. The chapel was used subsequently as a store for builder's materials, and then passed to a succession of independent Ministers, the Evangelical Association purchasing it in 1808. In 1882 the Congregational Church replaced it by the present Memorial Hall, containing a room capable of holding 500 people and nine classrooms. It was used as a mission hall until 1939.[5]

METHODISTS

John Wesley first preached in Wandsworth in November 1748: 'In the afternoon I preached to a little company at Wandsworth who had just begun to seek God, but they had a rough setting out. The rabble gathered on every side whenever they met together, throwing dirt and stones and abusing both men and women in the grossest manner. They complained of this to a neighbouring magistrate, and he promised to do them justice; but Mr C. walked over to his house, and spoke so much in favour of the rioters that they were all discharged'. Wesley noted that a few days later Mr C 'while walking over the same field, dropped down and spoke no more!' Mr C was Thomas Cawley, Vicar of Wandsworth, and the field was North Field.[6] Wesley began to refer to Wandsworth as 'this desolate place'.

In 1759 he baptised at Wandsworth two black servants at the house of Mr Gilbert, 'a gentleman lately come from Antigua', describing one of them, a woman, as 'the first African Christian I have known'. Gilbert later founded the West Indian Methodist Mission. The breakthrough came in the 1760s: in 1769 Wesley could write that 'The people here were the most dead, but are now the most alive of any about London'. In February 1770 he was at Wandsworth again: 'Every one thought no good could be done here. We have tried for above twenty years. Very few would even give us a hearing, and the few that did seemed little the better for it. But all on a sudden crowds flock to hear, many are cut to the heart, many filled with peace and joy in believing, many long for the whole image of God. In the evening, though it was a sharp frost, the room was as hot as a stove, and they drank in the Word with all greediness'. Wesley last preached at Wandsworth in 1790, and by then the Methodists had acquired their own chapel in the High Street. Their later church on

123. *The Methodist Chapel, possibly of 1772. It was next door to the Friends' Meeting House on the east side. From 1867 to 1959 it was used by the Primitive Methodists.*

East Hill, built in 1864-5, was destroyed in 1941 and replaced by a new church on the same site in 1957.[7]

Wandsworth had an Independent congregation by 1758. The Independent congregation which took over the French Chapel built their present church on East Hill in 1859-60. The Strict Baptists built a chapel in Fairfield Street in 1821, and replaced it with their present church in Haldon Road, West Hill (formerly a skating rink) in 1881.[8]

NINETEENTH-CENTURY EXPANSION

In 1819 the parish successfully applied for some of the funds provided to build new churches to commemorate the victories of Waterloo and Trafalgar, noting that the limited number of free seats in All Saints was 'most especially detrimental to the morals of the lower classes, who from the want of free seats are almost totally excluded from their parish church'. St Anne's Church, designed by Sir Robert Smirke and sometimes referred to as the pepperpot church, was completed in 1822, when workmen climbed to the top of the tower and drank the health of the church with a mug of beer. St Anne's became a separate parish in 1850. Because the Vestry and the bishop could not agree on whether the churchyard should have a fence or railings, no burials ever took place there.[9]

The third Anglican church was the result of private charity: Joshua Stanger, a retired business-

124. St Anne's Church in 1848.

man living near St Anne's, built St Mary's
Summerstown at his own cost in 1835 (on the
south corner of Garratt Lane and Summerstown).
A new building was provided on a new site, in
Keble Street, in 1903-4.[10]

The Catholic Mission in Wandsworth was established in 1841 'to care for the poor Irish who
worked in the market gardens of Wandsworth',
and two years later there was a congregation of
300. At first, services were held on the first floor
of a cottage next to the George and Dragon pub
on West Hill, where, because of its proximity to
the public house, 'voices of people could be heard
during Mass and the smell of tobacco was strong'.
The first missioner was Father Antonio de Lima,
a refugee from Spain. In 1847 the Catholics were
able to build a chapel designed by Pugin, capable
of seating about a hundred, on the east side of the
Plain beside the Wandle. The mission had constant problems, due to the large area covered, lack
of money and the fact that its priests were often
foreign, but it nevertheless grew. One of the
priests had the foresight to acquire a large plot
of land on West Hill in 1884, and the present
church of St Thomas was built there over a long
period, construction beginning in 1893 and the
tower being completed in 1927.[11]

*125. St Michael's Church, Wimbledon Park Road, as
designed by E.W. Mountford, a prominent local
architect, in 1897. The tower was never built.*

126. *St Paul's Church, Augustus Road, in about 1890, with the present chancel (of 1888) but a temporary nave (of 1877). A proposed tower was never built.*

Despite Wandsworth's history of Nonconformity and the number of chapels, the Church of England remained dominant on the eve of suburban expansion. On the Sunday in 1851 when a census of church attendance was taken, 63% of the attenders were at Anglican churches, 31% at Nonconformist churches and 6% at the Catholic chapel.[12]

Wandsworth's growth altered the proportions, but the Anglicans could not be accused of making insufficient provision in bricks and mortar. Seven new churches were provided by 1908, in several cases preceded by a temporary building or mission church: Holy Trinity, West Hill (1863, with spire of 1888); St Paul's, Augustus Road (1888 and 1896); St Stephen's, Manfred Road (1881-2; since rebuilt); St Faith's, Ebner Street (1882-3; since rebuilt); St Mary Magdalene's, Wandsworth Common (1887-8 and later); St Andrew's, Garratt Lane (1889-90 and later); St Michael's, Wimbledon Park Road (1897 and 1905); and St Barnabas', Lavenham Road (1906-8).[13]

Charles Booth described the varying character of these churches in 1902. St Faith's served a poor area, and Booth noted that 'Upon the very shifting element that continually passes through St Faith's – here one day and gone the next – the Church can exert little or no influence; but the permanent residents are visited assiduously, and it is claimed that a larger percentage than usual attend the church or mission hall, and also that they show the results in changed lives'. At the other end of the social scale was Holy Trinity: 'This rich man's church is well attended, and is a gold mine from which funds are drawn for all the poorer churches round'. (Pew rents at Holy Trinity were not abolished until the early 1950s.)[14] Different again was St Stephen's, where the large congregation was 'Evangelical rather than parochial, being mainly drawn from those who abjure the High Church practices in some of the adjacent parishes'.

The Nonconformists and Catholics also built extensively, in Earlsfield and Southfields as well as central Wandsworth. Several new denominations arrived: the Baptists in 1859 (building a church on East Hill in 1862-3), the Presbyterians in Merton Road in 1873-4, the Salvation Army in 1879 and the Unitarians in 1882 (building a church on East Hill in 1885). The Salvation Army faced particular hostility, with regular battles at their weekly open-air services on Wandsworth Common.[15] Their present 'Citadel' in Ram Street was built in 1907. When another religious census was taken, in 1902-3, the Anglicans accounted for only 49% of attenders, the Nonconformists for 46% and the Catholics for 6%.[16]

127. *The Wesleyan (or Methodist) Church, built in 1864-5, on the eastern corner of East Hill and Spanish Road.*

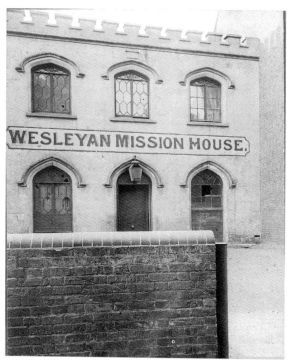

128. *Gothic House, Waterside, used by the Methodists as a mission hall from 1879 to 1898.*

MISSIONS

Wandsworth's churches made vigorous efforts to reach the poor. In 1902-3 there were nineteen mission halls (often 'iron churches') – some Anglican, some Nonconformist and some independent of any denomination, and generally in poorer areas such as the Wandle Valley and Waterside. The mission hall in Iron Mill Place was fairly typical in offering a Sunday school, mission services and (on weekdays) 'mothers' meetings, band of hope meetings, a working lads' club, a clothing club, a provident bank, &c.' Lindsay Glegg in 1905 entered the iron mission hall in Wardley Street and found 'a girl alone amidst thirty or more rough fellows aged from fifteen to twenty. They had come in to learn to read and write and to do sums on slates provided', following which hymns were sung.[17]

Booth was scathing about the failure of the missions and what he saw as the competitive bribery involved. However, much depended on the individual Ministers. Down Lodge Hall on West Hill, built in 1884 where the evangelists Moody and Sankey had begun their campaign in London in the previous year, had a tiny congregation in 1902-3, but was revived by Lindsay Glegg,

who served there for 45 years from 1917.[18]

Overall, the picture in 1902-3 was less gloomy than Booth indicated. Taking into account people who attended twice on a Sunday and the census organisers' estimate that about half the population was too young, too old, too busy or too sick to attend, just over one third (35%) of those who could have attended church did so, virtually the same proportion as in the London County Council area as a whole.

RECENT TIMES

Since then the number of worshippers has declined, the mission halls have disappeared and several churches have been rebuilt on a smaller scale. One new arrival was London's first mosque, built in Gressenhall Road in 1924-6. It was not the result of a Muslim community in Southfields but of the growth of a Muslim sect, founded in India in 1889 by Hazrat Mirza Ghulam Ahmad of Qadian, who claimed to be the promised Messiah. His son Mahmud later settled in Southfields, and died in 1965.[19] Another recent arrival is the Sikh temple at 142 Merton Road.

129. *A rare view of an 'iron church' – St John the Divine Mission Church, on the southern corner of Garratt Lane and Bendon Valley, probably in about 1910.*

130. *The mosque in Southfields shortly after its opening in 1926, showing Maulana Abdul Rahim Dard, the first Imam, with some visitors.*

Educating Wandsworth

Like many parishes, Wandsworth had a school connected with the church, with the parish clerk acting as schoolmaster. It is first recorded in 1551, when the churchwardens paid twelve pence for hinges for the schoolhouse door. The churchwardens confined themselves to repairs to the building and the school was probably supported either by fees or subscriptions, but from the 1630s the churchwardens also paid £2 a year 'for education of 4 poore boyes to make them fitt for apprentices'. The building was probably towards the north end of Garratt Lane: at the house attached to the Upper Mill in 1610 was a 'tiled barn adioyninge to the house there comonly called the Schoolehouse'.[1]

The school was put on a firmer footing by William Wicks, citizen and grocer of London, who left £200 in his will proved in 1715 to endow a free school for 25 children of the poor of Wandsworth, provided a further £300 was provided by others.[2] A site was obtained on the east side of Putney Bridge Road and the green coat school opened in 1720.

In 1813 the Rev. Philip Allwood, Wandsworth's curate, reformed the school on National School principles, whereby large numbers of pupils could be taught by senior pupils under a single master. Five years later it had 320 pupils. An education inquiry of that year concluded of Wandsworth that 'The poorer classes have sufficient means of educating their children'.[3] The school was rebuilt on the same site in 1820 and again in 1872, and continued until the late 1960s. The building of 1872, with later additions, still stands on the corner of Putney Bridge Road and Armoury Way.

There was also a school of industry for 40 girls from 1800 to 1866, partly supported (like the National School) by subscriptions from local people and sales of pupils' work. Its schoolhouse was on the western corner of the High Street and St Ann's Hill.[4] St Anne's and St Mary's Summerstown both acquired schools, and the former's on St Ann's Hill still operates as a Church of England primary school in its original building of 1858.

Other denominations also had their schools, notably the Quakers, discussed later. A British School, chiefly for Protestant Nonconformists, was founded in Point Pleasant in 1821 as the Wandsworth School for the Education of Children of every Religious Denomination. Fees were 'one penny per week ... from each child who is only taught to read, and an additional penny per week

131. The National School for girls of 1820, facing Putney Bridge Road on the site still occupied by later school buildings. The boys' school can be seen behind it. (Watercolour by E. Yates, 1825.)

132. St Anne's School in St Ann's Hill, as designed in 1858.

for writing, arithmetic, or needlework'. The purpose was not just to impart useful skills but to imbue 'moral and scriptural' principles ('devoid of sectarian principles'). In 1822 the school's committee noted 'that the conduct and behaviour of the children, generally in this place, have been strikingly improved since the establishment of this and similar Institutions', and that several of the poorer inhabitants 'have strongly testified their gratitude for the benefit received'.[5]

The school moved to a new building in Frogmore (opposite Sudlow Road) in 1868, was transferred to the London School Board in 1895 and closed in 1903. A Roman Catholic school opened in the Plain in 1842.

PRIVATE SCHOOLS

Wandsworth was typical of places around London in attracting privately-run schools. The Quaker schools are the earliest recorded. Richard Scoryer moved his Quaker boarding school from London to Allfarthing Manor House in 1696, offering to teach writing and arithmetic. It remained in existence until at least the 1790s. There were two Quaker schools for boys and several for girls in 1725. There was a French school for girls in 1725.[6]

Monsieur Pampillon's boarding school in the Upper Richmond Road attracted a remarkable clientele in the 1750s, including at least seven future peers. The Earl of Egremont, himself a pupil, recorded that Charles James Fox attended there for a year. The future Duke of Sutherland and Lord Grenville both attended a school on East Hill in the 1760s. In 1793 there were nine boarding schools or academies, including Mr Roberts's 'academy ... for the education of noblemen's sons' west of Wandsworth Common and James Chapman's 'good established academy for young gentlemen' on the western corner of Garratt Lane and the High Street. The latter was intended for the sons of wealthy merchants, and contained 'all the boys of the neighbourhood who were not intended for the learned professions'. There were 367 children at boarding schools in Wandsworth in 1792.[7] Private boarding schools still existed in the present century, notably Allenswood in

133. The Wandsworth School for the Education of Children of every Religious Denomination, just north of Prospect Cottages, Point Pleasant, drawn by E. Yates in 1825. The premises were used by the school from 1821 to 1868; they were later a mission hall.

134. Advertisement for Albion House School. The Rev. James Catts had a school in Garratt Lane in 1845.

Southfields up to the 1930s.

In 1818, in addition to boarding schools, there were 'a number of day schools, in which the children of the middle classes, and some of the lower classes of the inhabitants, receive education'. Several small independent schools are recorded in education returns of 1870, including those of Miss Eleanor Hills at 10 Tonsley Road with 25 pupils (regarded by the inspector as too crowded but having adequate instruction) and Elizabeth Stammer at 28 Smeaton Road, Southfields ('A small room with one small desk, crowded with children, 31 where there should have been 12. Failed utterly in arithmetic. Inefficient').[8]

One notable venture, established in 1855, was the Wandsworth Trade School, the first technical day-school in the United Kingdom. Its object was 'to provide instruction for the children of artisans and small tradesmen in the knowledge of common things, that may be turned to practical usefulness in after life. By the payment of eightpence or a shilling a week, children are taught a little of

135. In 1793 John Stedman's 'noted Academy for young gentlemen' occupied this handsome house of about 1700 on North Side (on the site now occupied by the underpass).

mechanics and chemistry, and the use of the steam engine, along with geography, history and arithmetic, and their bearings in relation to trade'. It was founded chiefly through the efforts of the Rev. James Booth, Vicar of St Anne's in 1854-9, Fellow of the Royal Society and Chairman of Council of the Royal Society of Arts. It used Albert House, Garratt Lane, and had 100 pupils in 1856, but, for reasons which are unclear, it closed in the following year.[9]

An important but poorly-documented institution was based in Garratt Lane, opposite the present Museum, and is marked on Stanford's maps from the 1860s onwards as 'Literary & Scientific Institution', though it was usually known as the Association Room. It was the premises of the Wandsworth Working Men's Association for Promoting Useful Knowledge. It is first recorded in 1838, and still existed at the end of the century.[10]

BOARD SCHOOLS AND OTHERS

London's School Board was set up under the Education Act 1870 to fill gaps in existing provision of elementary education. In the 33 years before its duties were transferred to London County Council (LCC) it built a fine series of schools, of

137. Waldron Road Board School, built in 1885 and destroyed by a bomb in 1940.

which those remaining are major landmarks. It first took over St Mary's Church Schools, Summerstown, in 1878, later replacing them by Waldron Road Board School (built in 1885). Its other schools were Warple Way (1880; now demolished), Eltringham Street (1886; now closed and partly demolished), Merton Road (1891; now known as Riversdale), Swaffield Road (1897),

136. A class in engineering sciences at Wandsworth Technical Institute in 1938.

138. *St Michael's School, Southfields, on Empire Day 1907. The school was moved from this iron building in Brathway Road to a new building in Granville Road in 1912.*

139. *Arithmetic using clay at Southfields School in 1907.*

VIEW FROM GARDEN

140. *The Convent of the Sacred Heart, on West Hill. The slightly lower building of five bays towards the right was the north facade of the mansion known as The Orchard.*

Brandlehow Road (1901; now rebuilt following bombing), Earlsfield (1903) and West Hill (1903).

Wandsworth Technical Institute was founded in 1895, on its present site, through the efforts of a local committee. Its purpose was to provide evening classes for technical education and a secondary school for boys and girls, and by 1900 it had over 1000 students. Its success led to considerable expansion: the present buildings facing the High Street were opened in 1926 and 1936, and others were added further south in the mid-1950s and the 1970s. It lost its remaining secondary school pupils in 1958. In 1972 it merged with Putney College of Further Education, and it is now part of South Thames College.[11]

New Church of England schools included St Michael's (1878) and St Faith's (1889). The Catholics established St Joseph's in Putney Bridge Road in 1875. The LCC continued to add new schools as the population increased, including the County Secondary School for Girls in 1907 (later known as Mayfield) and Riversdale County School in 1909 (subsequently incorporated in Southfields Comprehensive School).

Wandsworth had three teacher training colleges: that of the Society of the Sacred Heart on West Hill (1874-1905, after which the premises were a school), Southlands in Park Side (moved from Bat-

tersea in 1927 and now closed) and Whitelands in Sutherland Grove (moved from Chelsea in 1931).[12] In 1975 the latter two joined two colleges in Roehampton to form the Roehampton Institute of Higher Education, and the Institute's activities are now being concentrated on the Roehampton site.

MODERN SCHOOLS

The three main changes since 1945 have been the establishment of schools to serve the new Council estates, especially in Southfields, the creation in the 1950s of large comprehensive schools with up to two thousand pupils, and, more recently, school closures as the number of pupils has declined. The comprehensive schools (some new and some largely rebuilt) included Mayfield School (1956), Wandsworth School in Sutherland Grove (1957), Spencer Park School (1957) and Garratt Green School (1958; now Burntwood School). There were also Southfields School in Merton Road and John Griffiths Roman Catholic School (now Pope John Paul II School) in Princes Way. By 1990, the remaining secondary schools were Southfields, Burntwood and John Paul II. Some sites have been re-used for other educational purposes, such as Mayfield (closed in 1984) as a City Technology College since 1991.

The Poor and the Sick

CHARITIES

The parish provided its first 'howse for ye poore' (presumably almshouses) in 1569, described as being at the west end of the street. It was supplemented by twelve almshouses on East Hill in about 1627.[1] Henry Smith (1549-1628), one of the parish's greatest benefactors, left £500 to the parish to be invested in land to relieve the poor and provide work for them. Smith had been born in humble circumstances in Wandsworth, but prospered as a silversmith and became an Alderman of the City. Having no children, he left his large estate to a variety of charitable purposes. The parish appears to have spent the money sensibly in the ways Smith intended. In 1653, for example, it was used to buy hemp 'to sett the poore on worke', to buy broadcloth to clothe the poor, to buy wheat to make bread for the poor, to educate four children, to apprentice poor children and to relieve the poor, aged and infirm.[2]

Another important charity was founded by Francis Millington. He left £500 in his will of 1692 to provide a fund to support poor seamen or watermen aged 50 or more, born or dwelling in Wandsworth and who had lost limbs or been wounded at sea, and to provide them with blue great-coats. As late as 1899 there were 36 Millington pensioners, each receiving £4 a year, of whom fourteen were or had been seamen or watermen.[3]

THE WORKHOUSE

The parish workhouse was built on East Hill in 1730-1, using the site of the almshouses of a century earlier. It was supposed to supersede the giving of pensions and to discourage idleness. Under rules drawn up in great detail in 1748, work was to last from 6am to 6pm in summer and 7am to 5pm in winter. In summer, 'the healthy people and strong' were to rise by 5am, have breakfast at 8am, dinner at 1pm, supper at 7pm and be in bed by 9pm; half an hour was allowed for breakfast and an hour for dinner.[4]

When Sir Richard Phillips visited in about 1816:

'The matron conducted me into a spacious yard, round which are suites of rooms, built in the manner of alms-houses ... In the middle of the area stand the offices and kitchen, dividing it into two yards, one for men, and the other for the women. The

141. Monument to Henry Smith in All Saints Church.

whole had been recently white-washed, and, but for the name of work-house, and certain restraints on their habits and liberty, it seemed calculated to secure the comforts of its inmates. The matron took me into several of the men's rooms, and here I found tottering grey hairs, crippled youth, inveterately diseased of all ages, and artizans destitute of employment.'[5]

Shortly before, there had been another workhouse in the parish, belonging to St Mary le Strand, which hoped to be able to maintain its poor more cheaply in the country than it could in town. In 1768 it leased a house in Garratt Lane and contracted with a labourer, Edward Greening, to look after them. In 1792 there were 46 poor in the house. Soon after that the poor were moved back to town, the parish having decided (wrongly as it turned out) that, although costs were greater in town, this could be remedied by strict regulation.[6]

Under the Poor Law Amendment Act 1834, parishes could join together to form poor law unions. Wandsworth joined with Battersea and other neighbouring parishes, and the parish workhouses were replaced by a new and much larger one on St John's Hill, west of Usk Road (just outside Wandsworth's boundary), opened in 1838. Here in 1866

142. The parish workhouse, built in 1730-1, on the north side of East Hill east of the present Tonsley Hill. The lower buildings to either side were almshouses.

were 524 inmates, including 74 children. Eventually this was reckoned too small, and a huge new complex was constructed in Swaffield Road in 1885, capable of accommodating two or three thousand, apparently in the belief that an expanding local population meant a corresponding increase in the number of paupers. The old workhouse became an infirmary, known as St John's Hospital, and continued as a hospital until 1990. Part of it survives, converted to flats.[7]

The new workhouse was social engineering on a vast scale. Not only was there separation of men and women and of the aged and infirm and the able-bodied, but the able-bodied wards were divided into 'good and bad'. Working arrangements depended on the category; 'the worst class of women ... will be employed in absolute isolation, each in a washing cell', whereas 'the better' were to work in open stalls. One immense improvement was that quarters were provided for aged married couples, who had previously been separated.[8] In 1911 there were 874 people living in the workhouse, and another 256 in the workhouse school. The workhouse system officially ended in 1930, after which London County Coun-

143. The Horse and Groom pub, on the east side of Garratt Lane on part of what is now the Wendelsworth Estate. In 1900 local tradition was that the building had been a workhouse, and the land tax records and tithe map confirm that this was the workhouse of St Mary-le-Strand.

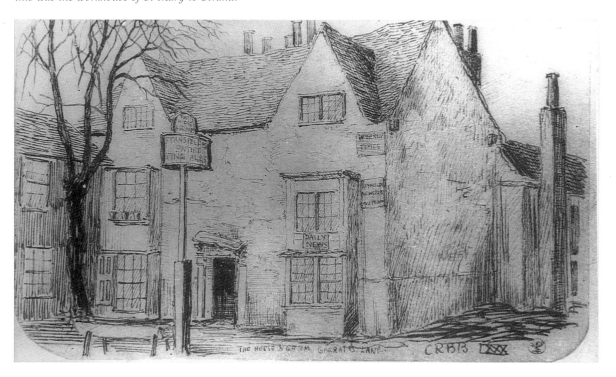

144 & 145. *Exterior view and one of the dining halls of the new workhouse, designed by Thomas Aldwinkle and built in Swaffield Road in 1885. It cost nearly £100,000. The centre block was of red brick with white stone facings; the other blocks were of yellow bricks ornamented with strings of red bricks.*

cil used the building as a men's hostel and gradually demolished it. In 1970 the site was redeveloped for housing and the Atheldene Centre.

ASYLUMS, ALMSHOUSES AND HOSPITALS

In the 1840s the southern part of Wandsworth parish was rapidly becoming a vast depository for the distressed or troublesome humanity of Surrey, the county's prison and asylum both being erected in that period. Wandsworth had the advantage that it was still largely rural, with large sites available relatively cheaply, and yet was close to London.

The Surrey Pauper Lunatic Asylum (now Springfield University Hospital) was built in 1838-41, at the southern edge of the parish. The site comprised about 97 acres, including farm land and gardens, and was later added to. In 1851 it accommodated 802 patients and 103 others – almost a tenth of the parish's entire population.[9] It was taken over by London County Council in 1899, becoming the Middlesex County Lunatic Asylum, and it remains a mental hospital today. Parts of the estate have been sold, including the site of the farmhouse (now occupied by Burntwood School), but most of the ancient Garratt estate remains intact in the hospital's possession.

St Peter's Hospital, or the Fishmongers' Almshouses, was a long-established City of London charity which moved to Wandsworth in 1851.

It was demolished in 1923, but the ornate gateway survives facing East Hill.

The Surrey Industrial School, for homeless and destitute boys not convicted of any crime, was established in 1853 in Bridge House, beside the Wandle. The aim was to prevent boys drifting into a life of crime. Until 1858, when government grants first became available, it was funded by a Miss Portal, who had been a leading figure in establishing boys' homes in Westminster and Kentish Town. 99 boys were being housed, fed and trained at the Wandsworth home in 1861. It was replaced later in the century by the Friendless Boys' Home, which had purpose-built premises on the corner of Spanish Road and North Side, designed to look like a terrace of six four-storey houses. At the back were workshops, a laundry, stables, engine houses and saw mills. It closed in 1902, but the building remains.

The Royal Hospital and Home for Incurables (now the Royal Hospital for Neuro-Disability) was inaugurated following a meeting in 1854, its purpose being 'the permanent care and comfort of those persons, above the pauper class, who by disease, accident or deformity, are hopelessly disqualified for the duties of life', as well as to provide pensions to those with incurable diseases. The hospital started at Carshalton, moved to Putney and finally in 1863 found its permanent home on West Hill, where numerous additions have been made to the Ruckers' mansion.[10]

146. The Surrey Pauper Lunatic Asylum, as built in 1838-41. It was designed by W. Moseley, the County Surveyor of Middlesex, and was of red brick, in 'Elizabethan' style, and 530 feet long. The building, much extended, still stands.

147. St Peter's Hospital (the Fishmongers' Almshouses) built on the north side of East Hill, next to the parish boundary, in 1849-51. It comprised 42 houses, each of three rooms, and a chapel.

148. The home for homeless and destitute boys at Bridge House in 1858. The house stood on what is now the western part of Young's Brewery, next to the Wandle.

149. The Assembly Room at the Royal Hospital for Incurables, part of the new wing built in 1879-81.

ROYAL VICTORIA PATRIOTIC ASYLUM

The Royal Victoria Patriotic Asylum was built with money from the fund for the relief of dependants of soldiers and sailors killed in the Crimean War. Patriotic fervour meant that the vast sum of £1 million was collected, much more than was needed. This embarrassing situation was resolved by using some of the money for an asylum for the 'education and training of three hundred orphan daughters of soldiers, seamen and marines who perished in the Russian War, and for those who hereafter may require like succour'.

A large site on Wandsworth Common was purchased from Earl Spencer, whose right to sell it was doubtful, and a huge gothic building was erected in 1857-9. The full complement of orphans was 300. At first the girls' education was designed to prepare them for domestic service, which had the beneficial financial effect that no staff had to be employed for cleaning, cooking and laundering, but this was gradually superseded by conventional schooling.

A similar institution for orphan boys was established in East Hill House and moved in 1872 to new premises on the northern part of the Wandsworth Common site (just outside the parish). However, it ran into financial difficulties, and the building was sold in 1883 to Emmanuel School, which still occupies it.

During the First World War the Asylum was used as a hospital. Numerous huts were added, and it eventually housed 1800 patients. The orphans finally left in 1938, a small school being established in Hertfordshire and eventually closing for lack of orphans in 1972. During the Second World War the building became an internment camp for aliens and a clearing house and interrogation centre for refugees from Europe. After the war it housed a succession of schools, the last of which, Spencer Park, left in 1976. The building's future was then extremely doubtful, and its condition rapidly deteriorated. It was saved by a businessman, Paul Tutton, who conceived the ambitious and high-risk, but eventually successful, plan of converting it to luxury flats, graphic and design studios, craft workshops and rehearsal studios.[11]

150. (Top) The dining hall in the Royal Victoria Patriotic Asylum in 1857. The hall is now used as a dance and theatre studio.

151. (Left) The Royal Victoria Patriotic Asylum, designed by Major Rohde Hawkins and built in 1857-9, seen from west of the railway cutting. The windmill was built in about 1837 to pump water into the Black Sea, a pond on what is now part of Spencer Park, following the construction of the railway cutting. The Black Sea was filled in in the 1870s and the windmill lost its sails, but the rest of the structure is still there.

Wandsworth Prison

Wandsworth Prison was originally the county gaol for Surrey. In 1847 the Surrey magistrates were worried by gross overcrowding and fever in the existing county gaols and wished to introduce the 'separate system', already in use at Pentonville, under which prisoners were prevented from having any contact with each other. They also hoped to save money by replacing their three small prisons with one large one. They decided to build a large new prison, within a mile of a railway station and not more than six or eight miles from London. Land at Wandsworth was purchased in the same year, construction began in 1849 and the prison opened in 1851. As built, there were 708 cells, together with 24 reception cells, 22 punishment cells and fourteen large rooms for 'misdemeanants of the first class'. There was room for extension

so that 1000 could be accommodated and a separate building accommodated female prisoners. The architecture was criticised in 1862 as 'mean and ill-proportioned to the last degree', with 'none of the austere impressiveness that should belong to a building of a penal character'.

The regime at Wandsworth was rigorous. Its aim was to separate prisoners from other criminals and expose them to influence by staff and prison chaplains. Prisoners spent the day in almost total solitary confinement, working, eating and sleeping alone in their cells with only an hour's exercise a day. Outside their cells they wore masks, except in the chapel. The separate system ruled out tread-wheels for hard labour, and instead crank machines with handles were used. The handles had to be turned thousands of times a day, entirely unproductively. From these, prisoners sentenced to hard labour progressed to pumping classes, whereby 36 prisoners, each in a separate compartment with a separate crank, delivered 6000 gallons of water a day to tanks on the roof.

The Prison Act 1877 brought Wandsworth and

152. Aerial view of the prison from the south-west in about 1925. The section to the right, with three radiating wings, was originally for female prisoners.

153. *The chapel, arranged on the separate system, whereby inmates could not see each other but all could see the Minister. This view, of an 'adult school', shows only some of the 422 separate stalls.*

155. *A cell in 1861, with a prisoner engaged in crank labour.*

all other prisons under government control. New regulations put an end to the separate system, which had been found to drive some inmates to madness and suicide. Female prisoners ceased to be accommodated by 1893. Another change was that, following the closure of the prison in which most of Surrey's executions had been carried out, executions began to take place at Wandsworth. Among those executed at Wandsworth were William Joyce (Lord Haw Haw) in 1946, John

George Haigh (the Acid Bath murderer) in 1948 and Derek Bentley in 1953. The last execution at Wandsworth was in 1962, two years before the last in the UK.

One of Wandsworth Prison's most famous inmates was Oscar Wilde, who spent the first six months of his sentence there. In the First World War the prison housed conscientious objectors and military criminals. Very few prisoners have escaped from Wandsworth, but it was the scene of one of the most famous escapes, that of the train-robber Ronald Biggs, with three other prisoners, in 1965.

The prison currently has about 900 prisoners and 540 staff, and follows a strictly-timed routine from breakfast at 7.30am to locking up at 8.15pm. About 230 prisoners are on remand and 275 are vulnerable prisoners, housed separately, but almost all the rest are held at Wandsworth only temporarily while awaiting allocation to prisons elsewhere.[1]

154. *The main gate to the prison. The Governor's house was to the left and the chaplain's house to the right.*

156. Looking along West Side towards North Side in about 1880. In the distance is The Gables.

Open Spaces

COMMONS

Commons were not 'common' in the sense of being available for use by all local inhabitants. They were owned by the lord of the manor, but people who held land as tenants of the manor (copyholders) had certain rights in them, for example to pasture animals and gather wood for particular purposes, which meant that the lord of the manor could not treat them as his private property. This was complicated in Wandsworth by the existence of several manors.

   Common land could be enclosed if the lord of the manor and those with rights on it agreed to do so. Early enclosures in Wandsworth were usually where the land was useful for some specific purpose. For example part of the common land in the angle between East Hill and North Side was enclosed as a new burial ground in 1680. Hogmore Green was appropriated for wharves and warehouses in the eighteenth century. By far the largest enclosure was that of most of the West Common in the Spencers' Wimbledon Park in 1758 and 1782, for which Wandsworth Vestry obtained

£50 a year. The part of the West Common north of West Hill was enclosed for a new mansion in 1764.[1] On the East Common there were a few scattered enclosures prior to 1800. These, which existed by the 1740s, are now Heathfield Cottages and the northern part of Spencer Park; also some land was taken for houses and gardens on West Side.[2] The reason for the enclosure of the whole of Allfarthing Piece on the East Common in 1802[3] is less obvious, since it was used as market gardens and was only built on much later.

   The commons were more seriously threatened in the nineteenth century, as their whole area became valuable as building land. Also, the number of those entitled to pasture animals on them declined. On the other hand, their recreational and scenic value was increasingly appreciated. Garratt Little Green, partly occupied by the Surrey Iron Railway prior to 1846, was enclosed between 1849 and 1865, one of the first buildings there being the present Prince of Wales pub. However, it was enclosures on the East Common which roused the community to action.

157. *Wandsworth Common, drawn by S.H. Grimm in 1795, with Westminster Abbey and St Paul's Cathedral in the background.*

SAVING WANDSWORTH COMMON

Apart from Allfarthing Piece and the small enclosures already mentioned, the East Common remained intact until the 1830s. Unfortunately, unlike Clapham Common, surrounded by large houses and fiercely defended, there were few influential inhabitants around Wandsworth Common. The London and Southampton Railway cut across the Common between 1834 and 1838, and the West London and Crystal Palace Railway did the same in 1854. The latter took far more than it needed, and sold part to builders, resulting in the construction of Chivalry Road and other developments. Sales of twenty acres to St James's Westminster Industrial Schools in 1850 and about twenty acres to Mr McKellar of Wandsworth Lodge between 1848 and 1856 eliminated most of the Common south of Bellevue Road. McKellar claimed his enclosures were necessary because gipsies on the Common endangered his property, but, according to an opponent, 'he rather encouraged these encampments by giving the gipsies beer, and then made it an excuse for his enclosures'.[4] The most damaging enclosure was of 55 acres between the two railways, sold for the Royal Victoria Patriotic Asylum (RVPA) in 1857 – like the other sales without any provision for the land to be restored to the Common if no longer used for the intended purpose. There seem to have been no protests at the time, unlike in the case of St James's Westminster.[5]

By the 1860s the Common was little used for grazing, but was 'greatly resorted to by the inhabitants of the metropolis, the access by rail being remarkably easy and the fares low'. However, only 150 acres remained by 1868 out of approximately 400. As one of the campaigners, John Buckmaster, later put it, 'land-grabbers and jerry-builders would soon have joined hands on the last square foot of turf'.[6]

Neither a petition to Earl Spencer in 1863 nor appeals to the Metropolitan Board of Works in 1868 achieved anything; indeed the Board indicated that if it took over the Common it would sell more of it for building in order to defray the cost. A lawsuit was filed by James Smith Digby against Earl Spencer and others. Digby was one of the last copyholders, occupying a tumbledown cottage in the Chivalry Road area and making a living 'selling potatoes, brickdust and treacle'. He actually liked the Common being developed, since it brought more trade, but, having been plied with gin and tobacco by Buckmaster, was persuaded to sign a piece of paper placed in front of him. Unfortunately, when eventually brought into court, he told the whole story. In 1869 Buckmaster led about 2000 people in breaking down fences erected on part of the Common where Chivalry Road now stands, and there was direct action and legal proceedings, both unsuccessful, over Plough Green (now covered by Strathblaine Road) in 1870.[7]

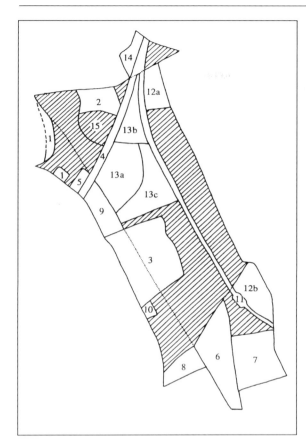

158. *Plan showing enclosures on Wandsworth Common, identified as follows: (1) pre-nineteenth century; (2) part pre-1740s, rest by 1838 (Mr Wilson's house); (3) 1802 (Allfarthing Piece); (4) c.1836 (LSWR); (5) 1836 (railway acquisition); (6) 1848-56 (Mr McKellar's enclosures); (7) 1850 (St James's Westminster Industrial Schools); (8) unknown date (granted on condition that it never be built upon); (9) 1852 (acquired by JPs to prevent it being built on); (10) 1852 (Telescope Piece); (11) 1854 (railway); (12a and 12b) 1854-62 (railway acquisitions); (13a to 13c) 1857 (RVPA; b sold to Emmanuel, c leased out); (14) 'by degrees', completed 1869 (Plough Green); (15) 1871 (Black Sea). The area remaining in 1870 is marked by diagonal lines.*

159. *The Rev. James Craig's telescope, for which Earl Spencer granted two acres of common land by Lyford Road in 1852. The telescope was said to enable a quarter-inch letter to be read at a distance of half a mile. Accounts differed as to how effective it really was, but Craig apparently became bankrupt. The site was restored to the Common under the 1871 Act.*

Of much greater importance were the formation in 1870 of a committee to contest Earl Spencer's claim to absolute ownership of the Common, and the contemporary struggle, also with Earl Spencer, over Wimbledon Common, together with the wider controversy about commons in general. Meetings about Wandsworth Common were held in Wandsworth, Battersea and Putney and at the Mansion House in London. The campaign was led by the wealthier inhabitants, but was strongly supported by the working people of Battersea and Wandsworth, several of whom addressed the first meeting in Battersea, and weekly subscriptions were raised at the various factories.

Eventually, probably influenced by the negotiations over Wimbledon Common, Earl Spencer agreed to a meeting with two members of the committee, which proved crucial:

'These two gentlemen spent an hour with Earl Spencer, discussing the question in a friendly spirit. Lord Spencer thought that as his income from the common amounted to £500 a year he was entitled to the annual receipt of that sum if he parted with his rights. Mr Ransome said he feared it was a larger sum than could be managed, and as the common was wanted for public purposes, he thought he might venture to fix upon £250 per annum as a sum that could be paid by the locality'.

WANDSWORTH COMMON

"E'en now the devastation has begun,
And half the business of destruction done.'

To the Inhabitants & Working Men
OF WANDSWORTH & BATTERSEA.

Will you allow Bankrupt and Speculating Builders, Land Societies, Beershop Keepers, Railway Companies, Tailors, Gentlemen, and Noble Lords, to rob you and your children of their
Common Rights and Footpaths, and the liberty of walking or
God's earth, without a struggle? During the last thirty years
enclosures have been made by the late Mr. W. Kellar and the
late Mr. Wilson, the enclosure for the Telescope, the enclosures by the Railway Companies, the Patriotic School, the
St. James's Industrial School, the enclosure by the Prison, the
enclosure by Mr. Costeker and Mr. Smith, making a total of
upwards of 200 acres! Most of these enclosures have been filched from
the Common and resold at an enormous profit.

WHAT'S THE REMEDY? Down with the Fences! Preserve
your Footpaths, show Lord Spencer and the Vinegar Men on the Board of
Works, who have neglected their duty, that you are determined to main
tain your rights like true Liberals and keep them like true Conservatives

Follow the Noble Example of Mr. Augustus Smith, who destroyed three miles of Fence on Berk
hampstead Common; the Men of Wigton who broke down the Fences erected by the Earl of Galloway
The Men of Buckinghamshire who broke down the Fences on Northall Common; the Men of Surre
who broke down the Fences on Shalford Common, and so Preserved their Rights!

Men of Battersea and Wandsworth, GO AND DO THOU LIKEWISE!
Cursed is he who removeth his neighbour's Landmark, and robbeth the poor of his inheritance
and joineth land to land to increase his riches.

DOWN WITH THE FENCES!

160. *Poster of 1870 calling for direct action. Crowds
assembled to break down fences at Plough Green (now
covered by Strathblaine Road) on 13 April 1870.*

Subsequently, after difficult negotiations, £250
per annum was agreed, provided that Spencer
could enclose the Black Sea (now the southern part
of Spencer Park). The final stage was to obtain
an Act of Parliament to effect the agreement and
establish independent conservators, against opposition from the Metropolitan Board of Works, which
now wanted to manage the Common itself. The
Act was obtained in July 1871.

The Conservators' duties were 'to keep the
Common for ever open and unenclosed and unbuilt
on ... for purposes of health and unrestricted
exercise and recreation'. The Common was in a
bad state, with stinking ponds, disused gravel pits
full of rubbish, no paths, muddy ditches, piles of
rubbish and 'every conceivable nuisance; the resort
of gipsy vans and tents and naked women washing their clothes in the said ponds'. The Conservators did much to improve it, particularly by
planting trees. Subsequently, the feeling that local
people were paying twice for commons (to the
Board in respect of London commons in general
and to the Conservators for their own Common)
resulted in control being transferred in 1887 to the

161. *Sheep grazing on Wandsworth Common near
Bellevue Road. These sheep were apparently part of the
experiment prior to 1921 in grazing Highland sheep on
Wandsworth, Clapham and Tooting Commons.*

Metropolitan Board of Works and thus eventually
to Wandsworth Borough Council.

The RVPA leased out its twenty-acre farm from
1885, and was suspected of intending to build on
it. However, the LCC bought the twenty acres in
1912, and later restored it to the Common, with
the farmhouse adapted as a refreshment room. In
1952 the LCC bought the remaining part of the
RVPA site, and used ten acres of it for housing
in the most damaging possible way, building the
high-rise blocks of the Fitzhugh Estate, completed
in 1955. Sale of the RVPA building and the land
around it to developers in 1994 has resulted in
further building but also some addition of land
to the Common. Recent controversies have been
over proposals to develop the ten acres opposite
the prison, bought in 1861 by the Surrey justices
(probably to ensure the security of the prison), and
over issues such as cycle tracks on the Common.

Garratt Great Green seems to have been forgot-
ten during the struggle for Wandsworth Common,
and remained under Earl Spencer's control. In the
1880s he was leasing it to several cricket clubs. The
LCC purchased it in 1899.[8]

PARKS AND GARDENS

In 1897 the LCC decided to acquire what is now
Wandsworth Park as an open space. It was then
occupied by market gardens and rubbish dumps
and was one of the few remaining undeveloped
areas in the north of the parish. Funding came
from the LCC, Wandsworth District Board and
public subscription. The land was levelled and
was laid out very much as it is today, though the
bandstand has disappeared. It was opened in
1903.[9]

The Mayor of Wandsworth, William Lancaster,
told the Council in 1902 that he proposed to lay

162. *Looking from near the junction of Merton Road and Buckhold Road across what is now King George's Park towards the paper mill on the Wandle in 1900.*

163. *The swimming pool in King George's Park in 1967. It was in use from 1938 to 1994.*

out two acres of land he owned in Southfields as a recreation ground, including a gymnasium for the young, and to hand it over to the Council 'as a Coronation Gift' if the Council would agree to maintain it as an open space for ever; his sisters wished to add the gift of a drinking fountain. The offer was eagerly accepted, and the land is now Coronation Gardens. Garratt Park, near Wandsworth's southern boundary, was opened in 1906.[10]

In 1915, prompted by plans to build on the remaining part of Wimbledon Park and to drain the lake, Wimbledon Corporation purchased what was left of the park, including the part in the Borough of Wandsworth, and this remains an open space.[11] A remarkable survival at the north end of the park is Horse Leas Wood, which existed before the land was emparked in the 1750s.

The decision to create King George's Park, together with Council housing on the higher land adjoining, was taken in 1921, partly in order to alleviate local unemployment. The land consisted of fields and a rubbish tip. It was to have been called Southfields Park until arrangements were made for King George V to open it in 1923. Further land south of Kimber Road has been added subsequently.[12]

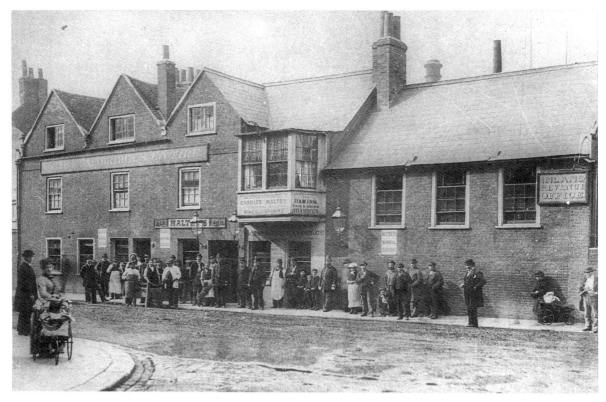

164. The Ram Inn, probably in 1882. It was rebuilt in 1883.

Wandsworth at Play

PUBS

Three of Wandsworth's public houses were regarded as inns, rather than mere alehouses, in the early nineteenth century – the Ram, the French Horn and the Spread Eagle. The Ram dated back at least to 1550, and was an inn by the early seventeenth century. The Half Moon (later the French Horn and Half Moon) on East Hill is first recorded in 1668. The magistrates sometimes held their Petty Sessions there in the eighteenth century. But it was the Spread Eagle, first recorded in 1664, which became pre-eminent. It was described in 1793 as 'the most principal inn in this town, and at which the gentlemen of the neighbourhood hold their societies or weekly meetings. Here is a pleasant coffee-room, facing the principal street; also at the back of the house there has been a spacious assembly-room lately erected, at which the gentry of the village, and its environs, hold their balls, assemblies, &c.'.[1]

The Spread Eagle's Assembly Room was used for all important local meetings, including annual meetings of Surrey Iron Railway shareholders and meetings to establish the British School, to create a gas company and to preserve Wandsworth Common. Earl Spencer's agent collected rents at the Spread Eagle in the 1820s, the Vestry held parish referendums there in the 1840s, the County Court was held there in the 1850s and the Baptists held services there from 1859 to 1863 until their chapel was built (as did the Methodists and Catholics at various times). The Assembly Room was rebuilt in 1890 and the rest of the inn in 1898. It retains much of its Victorian wood and glasswork.[2]

The number of pubs licensed in Wandsworth was restricted to 22 from 1786 to 1830, and virtually the same pubs were licensed at both dates.[3] They were clustered thickly in the village, including Waterside, the only exception being the Leather Bottle at Garratt. Some of the 22 already had long histories. For example, the Swan in the High Street is mentioned in 1550, the Antelope in the High Street in 1658 (as the Red Lion), the Ship in 1662,

165. *The Spread Eagle in about 1880.*

166. *The Old Bull and adjoining buildings, on the north side of the High Street by the bridge over the Wandle, probably in the 1880s.*

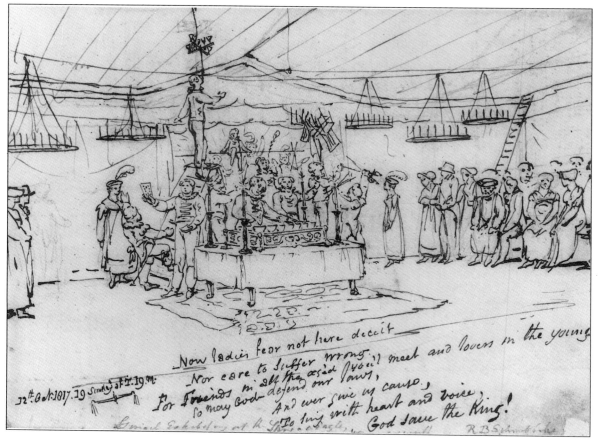

167. The Assembly Room in October 1817, with some sort of entertainment in progress, drawn by R.B. Schnebbelie.

168. The Waterman's Arms, just west of the Ship. It closed in about 1910.

169. The White Horse, Waterside, in about 1900, shortly before the site was absorbed into the gas works. The photographer is looking west along Waterside.

170. (Above) The Feathers, by the Cut north-east of the Causeway bridge. It closed in about 1888, but the building survived within a council refuse depot until 1959.

171. (Right) A beershop, the Old House at Home in Point Pleasant. It existed by 1867, and closed in about 1911.

172. (Bottom right) The Park Tavern, Merton Road, in about 1912, when it was a horse-bus terminus.

the Queen Adelaide in Putney Bridge Road in 1706 (as the King's Head) and the Crane, the King's Arms, the Leather Bottle, the Old Sergeant and the Rose and Crown in 1721. The survivors of the 22 are the Crane (whose name almost certainly referred to a crane on the Wandle), the King's Arms, the Leather Bottle, the Old Sergeant, the Queen Adelaide (renamed in about 1830 in honour of William IV's Queen), the Ram, the Rose and Crown (now Gleeson & Sons' Corner House), the Royal Oak, the Ship, the Spread Eagle and the Two Brewers (now The Brewers). No others date back before 1830. The Leather Bottle, the Crane and possibly the Old Sergeant still have premises dating back before 1830, though the Crane was partly rebuilt in the 1920s.

Licensing regulations were relaxed by the Beer Act of 1830, under which anyone could turn their house into a beershop without the need for a licence. Wandsworth had sixteen beershops by 1838, and many present-day Wandsworth pubs originated as beershops. They included the Winning Post in Garratt Lane, the Volunteer in the Plain, the Good Intent and the Foresters in Point Pleasant, the Barge Aground in Waterside, the Old House at Home at Dunt's Hill, the Hop Pole in Putney Bridge Road, the Corner Pin in Summerstown and many others. The name of the Waggon and Horses in Garratt Lane (first recorded in 1851 but probably existing earlier) may be a reference to the Surrey Iron Railway. A surviving beershop, in existence by 1853, is the Wheatsheaf in Putney Bridge Road, still with only one bar.

The first full licences for new houses were granted in 1849, one of the recipients being the Grapes, which was already a beershop by 1833. Most of the new licences were for substantial houses serving the newly-developed districts in the south of the parish, including the County Arms in 1852, the Park Tavern in 1853, the Prince of Wales in 1855, the Surrey Tavern in 1865, the Alma (commemorating a Crimean War battle, and retaining much of its Victorian interior) in 1867 and the Grosvenor Arms and the Lord Palmerston in 1868.

Many of the older houses were rebuilt in the late nineteenth century, notably the Ram in 1883, the Spread Eagle in 1898 and the Two Brewers in 1900. So were some of the newer houses, such as the County Arms in 1890. In the twentieth century many of the smaller houses have disappeared, either through loss of their licences or slum clearance or other redevelopment. All of those by the Thames, except the Ship, closed as a result of expansion of the gas works. The few new post-war pubs include the Jenny Lind in Inner Park Road, Southfields.

173. Wandsworth Baths, on the south side of the High Street west of the Wandle bridge.

THE SWIMMING BATHS

Wandsworth's public baths were built in the High Street in 1900-1. They included individual 'slipper baths', an important amenity for working-class inhabitants lacking a bathroom. There were 36 of these for men and twelve for women, and they were still in use in 1960. There were two large swimming baths, the larger one designed to be floored over in winter and used for gymnastics and public entertainments. Water was at first supplied from the mains, but later from an artesian well.[4] The baths were replaced by new ones at Putney in 1968, and the site is now part of the Arndale Centre.

THEATRES AND CINEMAS

The Spread Eagle's Assembly Room was licensed for concerts and music hall acts from 1859, and must have been the Wandsworth Theatre of Varieties recorded in South Street in 1902. In 1908 it was converted to a cinema – the earliest docu-

174. Advertisement for the Picture Palladium. The former Assembly Room appeared in directories under that name from 1912 to 1914.

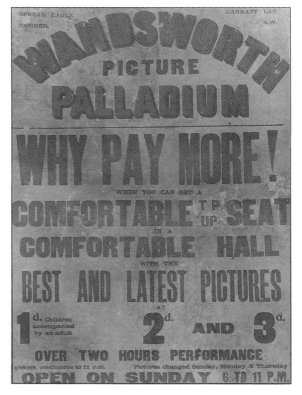

175. *The Premier Electric Theatre in Algarve Road, Earlsfield. It was built in 1910, renamed the Rex in 1950/1, closed in 1960 and demolished in 1988 after a period as a bingo club.*

mented architect-designed cinema scheme in London. It was known successively as the Biograph Theatre, the Picture Palladium and the Court Cinema. It closed in 1931, but the building remains, having been used for many years for storage.[5]

Seven other cinemas have existed in Wandsworth. From the earliest days of the cinema were the Central Hall Picture Palace of 1909 on East Hill, which lasted only until 1918; the short-lived Southfields Palace Cinema on the corner of Standen Road and Merton Road in about 1909; the Premier Electric Theatre in Algarve Road, Earlsfield (1910-60); and the Lyric Picture Playhouse in Wandsworth High Street (c.1913-1935). The Wandsworth Palace (later the Palace and the Gaumont) in the High Street opened in 1920 and closed in 1961, since when it has had an exotic career: a bingo hall from 1961, then a gospel church from 1982 to 1991 and currently a night club. The Lyceum Theatre in Southfields of 1920 was partly rebuilt in 1936, when it was renamed the Plaza Cinema; in 1968 it became a bingo club. From the great days of the cinema in the 1930s was the Savoy in York Road, seating 2153, opened in 1932 and sparking debate about whether a cinema of West End standards was suitable for such a poor area. The Savoy closed in 1959 and was demolished several years later.[6] Since 1968 Wandsworth has not had a cinema at all, but there are plans for an 18-screen cinema in the Arndale Centre.

176. *The Lyric Picture Play-house in the High Street west of All Saints Church. It was in existence by 1913, and closed in 1935.*

177. *Wandsworth Stadium in 1933. From left to right are King George's Park, the stadium, the Upper Mill's millpond and Garratt Lane.*

WANDSWORTH STADIUM

Wandsworth Stadium was north of King George's Park, on a site now covered by the Arndale Centre. It was opened in 1933 and could hold 20,000 people entirely under cover. That number attended a Borough Thanksgiving Service there for King George's Silver Jubilee in 1935. Greyhound races were held every week on Tuesday, Thursday and Saturday at 8.15pm, the dogs being kept and trained at Sunbury. The last race meeting was in June 1966.[7]

SPORT

The earliest references to sport in Wandsworth are to players of stoolball (a cross between cricket and rounders) in 1608-9 and to seven men who were fined 24 shillings in 1658-9 for being 'football players on ye Lords day'. There are references to cricket from 1750, and it was later played both on Wandsworth Common and Garratt Green.[8]

178. *Advertisement for a foot race in 1862. Copenhagen Grounds have not yet been identified. They were said to be able to hold 30,000 spectators, including an 'Arena' for '5,000 Ladies and Gentlemen who may wish to be select'.*

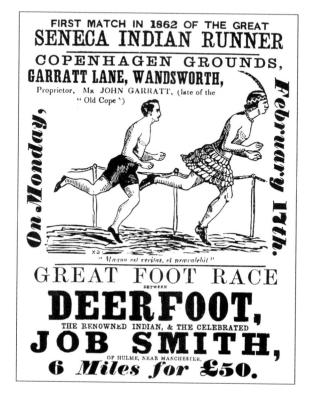

FIRST MATCH IN 1862 OF THE GREAT
SENECA INDIAN RUNNER
COPENHAGEN GROUNDS,
GARRATT LANE, WANDSWORTH,
Proprietor, Mr JOHN GARRATT, (late of the "Old Cope")

On Monday,   February 17th.

"Magna est veritas, et prævalebit."

GREAT FOOT RACE
BETWEEN
DEERFOOT,
THE RENOWNED INDIAN, & THE CELEBRATED
JOB SMITH,
OF HULME, NEAR MANCHESTER,
6 Miles for £50.

179. Southfields Rifle Club in about 1902. It was by the District Railway south of Granville Road.

Wandsworth has never had first-class teams in any major sport, but there are a few long-established sports clubs, such as the Heathfield Club of 1875 (originally a cricket club), Southfields Lawn Tennis Club of 1884 in Gressenhall Road (the oldest tennis club in London still at its original ground), and the South London Bowling Club of 1900 in Lyford Road (co-founded by W.G. Grace after his retirement from cricket). Several football grounds have existed, the earliest being Wandsworth football field west of Garratt Green, but most have been built over, including Summerstown football ground on the site of the Henry Prince Estate. Gover's Cricket School on East Hill existed from 1928 to the 1990s.[9]

180. Southfields Football Club, c.1905.

BALLOONING

Wandsworth became a popular launching point for balloons in the 1880s, probably because cheap gas was available. Leslie Bucknall in 1906 broke the long-distance record which had stood since 1836 by piloting his balloon from Wandsworth to Vevey on Lake Geneva, a distance of 400 miles.

A balloon called the Mammoth, 60 feet in diameter and carrying fourteen passengers, intended to break the long-distance record by reaching Russia, had a test run from Wandsworth gas works in 1907. Airships were launched from the gas works in 1908 and 1910.[10]

New Industries for Old

GAS

As long-established industries such as dyeing and calico-printing departed, new ones, usually with less specific reasons for being in Wandsworth, started to take their place from the 1830s. The one which had the greatest impact on Wandsworth was the manufacture of gas. The gas company was formed in 1834, and in the following year opened its works on the west side of Fairfield Street, just south of where the railway now runs (where the last remaining gasometer currently stands). Demand for gas gradually increased, and land north of the railway was first purchased in 1864. By 1912 the gas works occupied the whole

of the Thames-side between the Cut and the tramway depot, extending inland as far as Warple Way, and a large part of historic Wandsworth, including virtually the whole of Waterside, had been swept away.[1]

A smaller gas works was established in 1847 by John Dormay, in what is now Dormay Street, to supply himself and Wentworth, and he was soon supplying others as well. He stated that 'I have no foreman. I am my own master, engineer, inspector and everything'.[2] The larger firm bought him out in 1873.

Much of the company's success derived from the efficiency with which it handled the coal it used to make gas, which in turn depended on expansion to the Thames-side instead of using the Cut. In 1906 coal was first delivered by a collier rather than the less efficient barges, and in 1909 the company commissioned the first of its own steam colliers to bring coal direct from Newcastle to Wandsworth. In 1907 the company's gas was the

181. *Wandsworth gas works from the air in about 1925, showing the enormous area covered between the Thames and the railway. The Wandle and the Cut are at the bottom.*

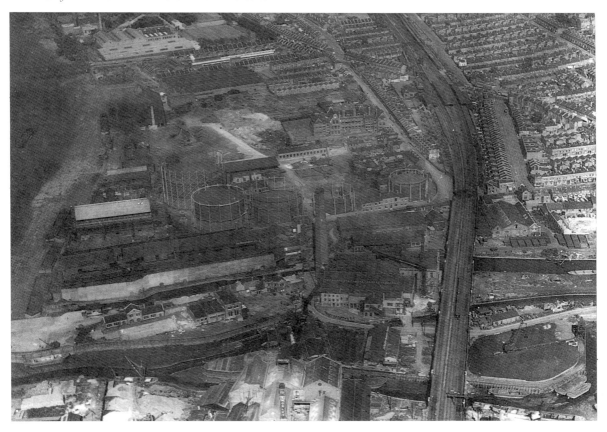

182. The new coal-discharging pier and hydraulic cranes at the gas works in 1934.

cheapest in London. Its first vessel, the *S.S. Wandle*, became famous in 1916 when it fought off a German submarine off the east coast; it had a triumphal reception all the way up the Thames from Gravesend to Wandsworth.

The company was notably paternalistic: a profit-sharing scheme was established in 1910, a Joint Works Committee (meeting monthly) to bring employees' concerns to the Board's notice shortly after the First World War and a pension fund in 1922. There were also sports grounds. The company was nationalised in 1949, and, with the introduction of natural gas from the North Sea, the works closed in 1971.

NEW INDUSTRIES

By 1867, in addition to paper-making, Wandsworth had acquired a chemical works, two colour manufacturers, a horsehair supplier, two artificial manure manufacturers and three lucifer and vesta (i.e. match) makers. There were also smaller trades and crafts, such as boat-building and coach-building.

Parchment was being made at Dunt's Hill, by the Wandle, in 1832. In the mid-1860s there were

buildings there described as 'Calico, Print, & Dye Works' and as a flock mill, and they were occupied by Thomas Townsend junior, colour manufacturer, and Roe & Co, horsehair manufacturer. The flock mill, which converted woollen rags into a soft substance like wool, lasted until 1940, though it abandoned water power by 1919 at the latest.[3] From about 1890 to 1928 Freeman & Son's Wandle Colour Works, on the east bank of the Wandle a little north of Mapleton Road, made all types of colours from those used by artists to those used by house painters, as well as varnishes and printer's ink.

There were several chemical works, including that of Messrs Hopkin and Williams, built near the gas works in 1861-2, where in 1898 they made 'all kinds of chemicals used for photography, and for the higher branches of chemical research'. In 1913 the company with others formed the Voelker Lighting Corporation with premises in Garratt Lane, Hopkin and Williams providing details of the process for using thorium compounds in gas mantle manufacture.[4]

Gas mantles were Wandsworth's main source of factory employment for women. Mantles were a sort of hood fitted over a special gas-burner: when the gas was lit, light was given off as the mantle's chemicals burnt. They were invented in 1884, and by 1900 four firms were operating in Wandsworth.[5] The last, Veritas, at 110-118 Garratt Lane, closed in 1972. The extensive premises of the Welsbach Incandescent Gas Light Co still stand in Broomhill Road. Another major source of employment for women was laundries.

Fireworks were made both at Riversdale Works, in the area now occupied by the Henry Prince Estate, from at least 1884 to 1902, and in the Osiers around the turn of the century. Both factories were a collection of scattered sheds, to ensure that any fire did not spread. Three young women were killed by an explosion at the Riversdale Works in 1888.[6]

The two factories which can still be seen in Eltringham Street and Petergate, north of the railway, were built in about 1892.[7] The smaller one was constructed for the Rainproof Cloth Co, which had developed a process for rendering cloth water-proof but not air-proof, and which moved from east London to these larger premises in order to meet orders from the War Office.

PIONEERS

Silas M. Burroughs and Henry S. Wellcome, whose business is now part of Glaxo Wellcome, had their first factory at Wandsworth, in Dormay Street. They were pharmacists from the United States, in partnership in London from 1880, and had established their business in much of the world by the

183. Employees of the Voelker gas mantle factory, Albert Works, 57 Garratt Lane, at the corner of Malva Road in January 1910.

184. From the 1870s Wandsworth increasingly attracted noxious trades forced out by suburban growth elsewhere. This view, of about 1900, is of Cole's fat-melting works, established in about 1895 on what is now Coronation Gardens, Southfields. The resulting products were used for manure, soap and candles.

185. *Burroughs, Wellcome & Co.'s first factory (and laboratories) at Wandsworth in the 1880s. It stood in what is now Dormay Street, apparently by Bell Lane Creek. The factory burnt down in 1889.*

end of the following year. To avoid stamp duty on the 'tabloids' (i.e. pills) which they imported from America, they set up their factory in Wandsworth to make them to a standard of quality and consistency previously unknown. Their lease at Wandsworth was for six years from 1883, after which they moved to larger premises at Dartford.[8]

Much of the early work on powered flight by A.V. Roe (Alliot Verdon Roe, 1877-1958) was carried out at Wandsworth. By 1906, he was spending much time at his brother's house, 47 West Hill (on the south side west of the fire station and now demolished). Here he made not only models, one of which won the *Daily Mail* prize for flying more than 100 feet, but also, in 1907, a biplane with a 30-foot wing span. William R. Daws, owner of a cycle business at the corner of West Hill and Lebanon Road, helped with small engineering and welding jobs, and may have obtained the engine. Roe drove the chassis up West Hill early one morning to test it on Wimbledon Common. In 1908-9 he constructed a

186. *Alliot Verdon Roe and his triplane, built at Wandsworth.*

187. APV's foundry on the west side of Point Pleasant in 1935.

188. The Frame Food factory in Standen Road, designed by W.T. Walker and erected in 1904, with art nouveau decoration by the artist Charles E. Dawson. Frame Food remained here until the late 1940s. The building survives.

triplane at West Hill and, unable to find anywhere to test it locally, obtained space on the Lea marshes in Hackney, where in July 1909 it achieved what is recognised as the first powered flight in Great Britain in an all-British aircraft. Roe established a factory in Manchester in 1910, and his firm, AVRO, designed some of the most successful aircraft of the two world wars.[9]

The Aluminium Plant and Vessel Co Ltd, which became the international company APV Holdings, was founded in a former malthouse on the east side of Point Pleasant in 1910. Richard Seligman, its founder, had acquired the rights to the technique for welding aluminium. By 1914 the company was established as a specialist fabricating firm supplying welded vessels mainly to the brewery and vegetable oil trades, with 60 employees. During the First World War it made equipment for explosives factories and petrol tanks for airships and aeroplanes. By the mid-1920s it was supplying complete plant lines and even whole factories, and was beginning to take over the entire Point Pleasant area, building a new foundry on the west side in 1930 and a new works on the east side in the late 1930s. During the Second World War nearly 3500 petrol tanks were made for Spitfires, and additional premises were acquired elsewhere in Wandsworth. The number of staff rose to 1400 in 1951. By this time the Point Pleasant site was too small, and the firm moved to Crawley in 1952-5.[10]

THE TWENTIETH CENTURY

Wandsworth's industries diversified further in the twentieth century. Apart from APV, notable new arrivals included Columbia Gramophone in Bendon Valley from about 1907 to 1932, Benham

& Sons, engineers (makers of cooking apparatus) on the site of the former Adkins Mill by 1914, the oil terminal at Point Pleasant from 1920 to 1990, Wandleside Cable Works, near Benham's, from 1932, Redifon Ltd in Broomhill Road from the 1940s to the 1980s, at first making radio equipment and later flight simulators for airline pilots, Airfix Industries in Haldane Place, Garratt Lane, from the 1950s to the 1970s, making plastic kits, and many others. There were numerous smaller engineering and electrical firms, and several making motor vehicles, such as Allan Taylor in Armoury Way.[11]

Most of the industry continued to be in the Wandle valley or beside the Thames, but additional areas of light industry developed in Merton Road and Standen Road. The area now known as Osiers Road, previously marshy, was developed for industrial use in 1912-20. Slum areas were converted to industrial use south of Wandsworth High Street and at Wardley Street, Lydden Road and Bendon Valley in the 1950s.

The post-war story, as elsewhere in London, has been industrial decline, including the closures of APV in 1952-5, the gas works in 1971, Benham's in the 1980s, Morganite Special Carbons in 1988 and Watney's distillery in 1989. APV's reason was the need for more space, though the move would have been risky had not Crawley Corporation offered housing for its employees, which enabled it to keep its skilled workforce together. Morganite found it increasingly difficult to find suitable people for factory work in Wandsworth. In the distillery's case, the development value of the land seems to have been crucial.[12] At Point Pleasant, industrial employment has been replaced by office employment; many other Thames-side sites are currently derelict.

Modern Wandsworth

BETWEEN THE WARS

Southfields and Earlsfield both had substantial undeveloped areas in 1918. It was in the latter in 1920-2 that Wandsworth Borough Council constructed its first estate, the Magdalen Park Estate, consisting of 376 houses between Openview and Swaby Road. Its next estate, 220 dwellings in and around Longstaff Crescent and Buckhold Road, was part of a larger scheme involving the creation of King George's Park, and was substantially complete by the end of 1925. A third scheme – 72 flats in Merton Road in Merton, Cumber, Acuba and Mastin Houses – began in 1929 and initiated the clearance of the Wandsworth Plain area by rehousing the inhabitants of Cumbers Yard (off Frogmore). A further 26 acres were acquired on the Magdalen Park Estate in 1931, now the area from Fieldview to Tilehurst Road, part of which was leased to private builders and part of which was used by the Council for 344 maisonettes, thereby completing the development of the area between Burntwood Lane and Magdalen Road.

Thereafter, much of the Council's emphasis was on slum clearance, especially in and around Wandsworth Plain. Armoury Yard, Hills Yard, Ash Tree Grove and Cumbers Yard were replaced in the 1930s by blocks containing 185 flats and a new road (Armoury Way) in the largest ever transformation of central Wandsworth. The Henry Prince Estate, named after the Housing Committee chairman from 1919 to 1936, was built in Garratt Lane in the late 1930s, with 272 flats, to help reduce overcrowding elsewhere.

London County Council's one estate in Wandsworth was the East Hill Estate, 524 flats on the site of the Fishmongers' Almshouses (since replaced themselves). The few private sector developments were in Earlsfield and Southfields, where Skinners Wood gave way to Combemartin Road, Skeena Hill and Girdwood Road in 1929.

Wandsworth Borough Council remained firmly Conservative until 1945, but the Wandsworth Central parliamentary constituency was marginal, being won by Labour in 1929 and 1937. Between 1940 and 1950 it was represented by Ernest Bevin, former trade union leader, prominent member of Churchill's war-time coalition Cabinet and Foreign Secretary in the Labour Government of 1945-51.

189. Queen Mary calling at 37 Longstaff Crescent, home of Mr and Mrs Waters, in 1923, on the day King George's Park was opened.

190. Building houses on the Council's Magdalen Park Estate in about 1920.

191. Single-storey slum dwellings in the Wandsworth Plain area in about 1930.

WAR AND REBUILDING

Bomb damage in Wandsworth was scattered rather
than devastating large areas.   The majority of
Wandsworth's flying bombs in 1944 fell in
Earlsfield and the St Anne's area.   Landmarks
destroyed included the Presbyterian Church in
Merton Road, the Methodist Church on East Hill,
the Alvering Library, Waldron Road School,
Brandlehow Road School, Wandsworth Fire Sta-
tion and the Bull public house in Wandsworth
High Street.

Slum clearance continued after the war, especially around Wardley Street, in the Iron Mill Place
area and in the alleys south of the High Street,
where the last to be occupied were Newtons Yard
in 1955 and Simrose Court in 1957.[1]   However,
most of the Council's major schemes involved
replacing large Victorian villas in substantial
grounds, especially in Southfields.   Temporary
pre-fabricated houses were also built, and some
of those in King George's Park and on Wandsworth Common remained until the 1960s.   The
main schemes were the Wendelsworth Estate (replacing slums and extended in the 1960s), three
sites in Portinscale Road, the Wimbledon Park
Estate between Albert Drive and Wimbledon Park
Road and the whole area between Beaumont Road
and Princes Way in Southfields.   Most of these
were completed in the 1950s.

Major estates built by London County Council,

*192. King George VI and Queen Elizabeth visiting
Armoury Way and the new Council flats on 16 March
1938. The new road's name came from Armoury Yard,
which was apparently named after the armoury used by
volunteer forces in 1745 and during the Napoleonic
Wars.*

193. *The Municipal Buildings. A new Town Hall had been built in 1926-7, and still stands as part of the Civic Suite. The Municipal Buildings were built in 1935-7, to the design of Edward Hunt. The stone reliefs portray incidents and industries in the history of the borough.   Subsequently, in 1973-75, the present Civic Suite was added.*

194. *Mrs Whitehouse's cafe in Point Pleasant in about 1935.*

195. *Damage at the junction of the Upper Richmond Road and West Hill following bombing on 21 October 1940.*

some including tower blocks, were the Aboyne Estate in Aboyne Road, Summerstown, the Ackroydon Estate in Princes Way, the Argyle Estate in Park Side, the Longstaff Estate on West Hill and the Trinity Estate (now the Fitzhugh Estate) in Trinity Road. The Borough Council's later schemes included the Arndale Estate in the late 1960s and the Orchard Estate on West Hill in the mid-1970s.

Much of Victorian and Edwardian Wandsworth remains, with the exception of the houses at each end of the scale – those categorised by Booth as 'wealthy' and, with a few exceptions, those categorised as 'poverty & comfort (mixed)' or worse. 'Gentrification' has occurred in some areas, especially around Tonsley Hill and Alma Road.

The most significant post-war change was in the people rather than the buildings. In 1991, about 15% of Wandsworth's population counted themselves as ethnic minorities, somewhat less than in the Borough or in Greater London as a whole (20% in both cases).[2] Politically there has been change too, especially the inauguration of the long period of unbroken Conservative control of the Borough Council in 1978, but this belongs largely to the story of the Borough rather than to that of Wandsworth itself. The 1991 census showed that Wandsworth lacks extremes of deprivation and wealth, at least once aggregated into wards.

TRAFFIC AND PLANNERS

Central Wandsworth only gradually became the huge traffic system it is today. The linking of York Road and Ram Street in 1906, the widening of Wandsworth High Street in about 1914 and the widening of East Hill in 1920-1 were all for the benefit of trams. Armoury Way was devised as a by-pass, though it passed through the middle of the Council's Wandsworth Plain Estate, and was completed in 1938. A one-way system had to await the elimination of trolleybuses, and eventually came into being in 1964. Recent proposals have been to make Armoury Way two-way again and restrict traffic in the High Street.[3]

The County of London Plan of 1943 proposed a series of new roads, including roads connecting Wandsworth Bridge with Trinity Road (eventually built), and a new south circular road (not built) from the foot of West Hill across King George's Park and the St Anne's area to Trinity Road and to a major roundabout on the southern part of Wandsworth Common. Even more destructive proposals were put forward in 1965 as part of a system of motorway boxes around London, and fortunately were defeated.

The largest development in central Wandsworth was the Arndale Centre of 1967-71, built by the Arndale Property Trust and taking in the sites of the greyhound stadium, the swimming baths and much else. It was to be the largest covered shopping centre in Europe, and included a large Council

196. The new Southfields in 1963, looking towards Park Side and Wimbledon Common. Whitlock Drive in the foreground was still under construction.

estate consisting of more than 500 flats in tower blocks directly above the shopping centre.[4] The result was one of London's great architectural disasters, though some of its shortcomings may now be dealt with by the Wandsworth Challenge Partnership.

The major planning opportunity of recent decades has been on the Thames-side, particularly following the closure of the gas works in 1971. The Greater London Council took over the site and prepared a scheme for industry and Council housing, which had to be abandoned following the discovery that the land was heavily contaminated.[5] Part of the site was used for the West London Waste Transfer Centre, but much of it is still derelict. There is currently an unprecedented opportunity to revitalise almost the entire riverside area and reincorporate it into the town, with plans under consideration for the sites of the oil terminal, Feathers Wharf, much of the gas works

and the distillery. The scheme already completed at Point Pleasant shows what can be achieved.

For much of the present century Wandsworth has suffered from a lack of identity, reflecting both the uncertainty about where Wandsworth begins and ends and the use of its name for a cobbled-together borough. Formation of the Wandsworth Society in 1971 has done something to remedy this. The initiative came from the eastern part of Earlsfield, where all but three of the original committee members lived. In 1997 committee members' residences were scattered around the old parish, though all but one east of the Wandle.[6] The Society campaigns actively on numerous issues. The twentieth century has in some ways been unkind to Wandsworth, and the more enlightened planning policies now followed and the commitment of local people offer the best hope of undoing past mistakes and making the most of Wandsworth's considerable advantages.

197. Nightmare scenario: the proposed Wandsworth Interchange in 1972.

198. The Arndale Centre from the north-west.

Notes

Abbreviations

Booth   C. Booth, *The life and labours of the people in London*, part 3, vol.5 (1902).

Coward   E.G. Coward, *Wandsworth and Putney* (1893).

DCR   LA, Dunsford court rolls.

Edwards   J. Edwards, *Companion from London to Brighthelmston* (1801, but relates to c.1793).

HH   Hand in Hand insurance policies, Guildhall Library, MS 8674.

HLRO   House of Lords Record Office (private bill evidence unless indicated otherwise).

LA   Lambeth Archives.

LMA   London Metropolitan Archives.

Loobey   P. Loobey, *The archive photograph series: Wandsworth* (1994).

NRO   Northamptonshire Record Office.

PP   *Parliamentary Papers*.

PRs   J.T. Squire (ed), *The registers of the parish of Wandsworth ... 1603-1787* (1889).

PRO   Public Record Office.

SAC   *Surrey Archaeological Collections*.

SRO   Surrey Record Office.

SRS   Surrey Record Society.

Sun   Sun insurance policies, Guildhall Library, MS 11936.

VCH   *Victoria County History - Surrey*.

WAM   Westminster Abbey Muniments.

WBN   *Wandsworth Borough News*.

WH   *Wandsworth Historian* (published by Wandsworth Historical Society).

WLHC   Wandsworth Local History Collection, Battersea Library.

WHNS   Wandsworth Historical Society News-Sheet.

WN   WLHC, Wandsworth Notes.

WNQ   *Wandsworth Notes and Queries* (1898-9).

WVM   WLHC, Wandsworth Vestry minutes.

Sources frequently used are cited at the beginning of each section below and not usually otherwise. No references are given where the source is clearly local directories or one of the following maps: Gardiner's map of Allfarthing Manor in 1633, drawn in 1640 (SRO, 3991/1); Rocque's map of the environs of London c.1745; Corris's map of Wandsworth 1787 (British Library, Althorp papers P13, part 1; book of reference in NRO, Spencer Surveys 1); Wandsworth tithe map 1838 (copy in WLHC); OS maps of 1865-6, 1893-4 and 1913.

Introduction

1. LCC, *Court minutes of the Surrey & Kent Sewer Commission* (1909), 10.
2. J. Blair, *Early medieval Surrey* (1991), 39-40.
3. NRO, SOX 211, Henckell case; PP 1852 vol.12, 766.
4. SAC vol.21 (1908), 179.
5. J. Aubrey, *The natural history and antiquities of the County of Surrey* (1719), vol.1, 14.
6. PP 1852 vol.12, 766.
7. WBN 27/10/1967, 3.
8. SAC vol.10 (1891), 248-9; LMA, prints (Burns cuttings); WHS Collection, 1543.

Early Wandsworth

Unpublished note by Pamela Greenwood on Wandsworth archaeology, 1998.
Barbara Harvey, *Westminster Abbey and its estates in the Middle Ages* (1977).
VCH vol.4, 110-14 (manors).
WH 53 (1987), 10-19 (fields).

1. WH 48 (1986), 6.
2. SAC vol.35 (1924), 125-6; WH 2 (1971), 6-7.
3. WH 2 (1971), 6-7.
4. WH 13 (1975), 4-5; C. Hailstone, *Alleys of Mortlake and East Sheen* (1983), 8.
5. WAM (Charter) 1; J.G. Taylor, *Our Lady of Batersey* (1925), 6, 20.
6. J.E.B. Gover *et al*, *The place-names of Surrey* (English Place-Name Society XI, 1934), 7, 36; WAM 1740.
7. J. Morris (ed), *Domesday Book: Surrey* (1975).
8. PRO, LR 2/197, ff.4-5.
9. B. Harvey, *Living and dying in England 1100-1540* (1993), 99.
10. DCR, 11 May 1570, 13 Dec 1571, 2 Nov 1576; SAC vol.18 (1903), 117-22.
11. PRO, LR 2/197, f.5; 1633 map; PRO, MR 1152.
12. WAM 27494-27691; WAM 50781, f.4.
13. WH 40 (1984), 8-12; WAM 27653-75.
14. Taylor, *Our Lady*, 310-11; WH 66 (1993), 10-11; SRS vol.11 (1932), 196.
15. SAC vol.15 (1900), 90-102; WH 63 (1991), 20-1.
16. SAC vol.49 (1946), 121-2.
17. Camden Society, 3rd ser., vol.8 (1905), xxviii, 4.

Stuart Wandsworth

WH 42 (1984), 15-22; WH 44 (1985), 8-14; WH 63 (1991), 1-5; WH 64 (1992), 5-7 (the Brodricks).
Allfarthing map 1633.

1. WH 16 (1977), 8-12; LMA, P95/ALL1/45, 1663-4.
2. PRs; P. Slack, *The impact of plague in Tudor and Stuart England* (1985), 151.
3. LMA, P95/ALL1/45, 1665-6, 1666-7; WNQ 15.
4. LMA, P95/ALL1/45, 1657-8; Lambeth Palace Library, E2/65; W. Rye, *Some notes on the deeds relating to the parish and other charities of Wandsworth* (1881), 31-6.
5. LMA, P95/ALL1/44, f.197 (mis-bound); WNQ 215-16.
6. SAC vol. 21 (1908), 170-91.
7. *Surrey Quarter Sessions Records: 1663-6* (1938), 9-10.
8. PRs; British Record Society, vol. 99 (1990).
9. PRO, E179/188/481; SRS vol. 17 (1940), xcii; WNQ 79-80.
10. PRs, p.127; LMA, P95/ALL1/45, rate list at start; NRO, SOX 277, 1705 lease to J. Workman.
11. Bodleian Library, Rawl C 984, f.258.
12. Huguenot Society *Proceedings*, vol. 1 (1887), 241.
13. *Calendar of State Papers Domestic*, 18 Nov 1695.
14. *Dictionary of National Biography*.
15. DCR 1681-91; *Notes & Queries* 12th ser. ix (1921), 141-3.
16. WH 50 (1986), 23-4.
17. DCR; Walpole Society, vol. 15 (1927), vol. 21 (1933), Vertue notebooks vol. 1, 84, 86-7; R. Gunnis, *Dictionary of British sculptors 1660-1851* (1953), 72-4.

Georgian Wandsworth

WVM.
1851 census.
N. Perry, *Sir Everard Fawkener: friend and correspondent of Voltaire* (1975).
T. Besterman, *Voltaire* (1969).

1. D. Lysons, *The environs of London* (1792), vol. 1, 511
2. LA, deed 5759
3. SRO Guildford, 145/Box 17, Extract Book 9, 10, 82-7; *ibid.*, Box 13, Blakiston auction; HH 19 p.277
4. SRO, 85/2/4/1 No. 112; LA, deed 5808; R. Milward, *The Spencers in Wimbledon: 1744-1994* (1996), 66.
5. SRO, QS2/6/1771 Mids 27-8; directories 1790s to 1832; WN vol. 1, 27; WNQ 248-9; WVM 1832, p.75.

6. British Library, Add 9436, f.375.
7. PRO, PROB 5/2026.
8. British Library, Add 9436, ff.21, 374; Thomas Milne's land use map 1800; WVM 27 May 1716, 8 June 1740.
9. British Library, Althorp Papers P13 part 1.
10. WH 44 (1985), 13.
11. NRO, SOX 439, copies of earlier documents; WVM 1831 p.60; PP 1901 vol. 51, 846.
12. NRO, SOX 261 (2).
13. *Ibid.*; WVM 1828, p. 611; *The Times*, 17/3/1828, 6e, 1/4/1828, 1f.
14. WH 44 (1985), 11; NRO, SOX 101, 1758 plan; WVM 6 Mar 1782; Milward, *Spencers*, 21.
15 NRO, Spencer MR, Wandsworth freehold rental, 1755 Williamson.
16 WNQ 36-7.

The Wandsworth Mills
C.T. Davis, *Industries of Wandsworth* (1898).
SAC vol.21 (1908), 170-91 (Wandle in 1610).
'Wandsworth's mills to 1700', WH (forthcoming).

1. Some of the names given are not those used in 1610.
2. VCH vol.4, 114; WNQ 54-7, 185; *Valor Ecclesiasticus* (1810), vol.I, 416; PRs 1624.
3. WHS Collection, 1543.
4. J. Aubrey, *The natural history and antiquities of Surrey* (1719), vol.1, 14; PRO, E 112/522, No. 225.
5. HH 34 p.160, 47 p.325, 60 p.174; WVM 1 May 1788.
6. *Institution of Civil Engineers, Minutes*, vol.20 (1860-1), 206.
7. WHS Collection, 1543; K.G. Farries and M.T. Mason, *The windmills of Surrey and inner London* (1966), 214.
8. HH 47 p.229, 50 p.353; Sun 209/300713; WH 11 (1974), 1-2.
9. WBN Handbooks (1911-13), No.1, 15.
10. WH 11 (1974), 3.
11. *South Western Star*, 30/11/1928, 7.
12. PRO, C 24/883, Roberts v. Wilkes; PRO, E 133/106/23; PRO, E 112/522, Nos.224, 255; PRs; WNQ 233.
13. PRO, E 112/522, No.224; Huguenot Society *Proceedings*, vol.1 (1887), 303; NRO, Spencer MR, Wandsworth freehold rental.
14. WHNS 1995/190.
15. D. Hughson, *London ... history and description of the British metropolis*, vol.5 (1813), 395; Sir Richard Phillips, *A morning's walk from London to Kew* (1820), 86-8.
16. NRO, SOX 211, Henckell case; WHNS 1995/190.
17. WVM, 1830, p.25; WH 50 (1986), 19-20.
18. *Ibid.*; WN vol.8, 103.
19. PRO, E 112/521, No.144; SAC vol.83 (1996), 126, 133n.
20. *Ibid.*, 129; Senex's map of Surrey 1729; Rocque's map 1740s; HH 78 p.290, 91 p.149, 103 p.281, 107 p.348, 117 p.225, 125 p.302: ICE, *Minutes*, 204.
21. Phillips, *Morning's walk*, 84-5.
22. WH 50 (1986), 20; OS map 1893-4; Davis, *Industries*, 5; C.T. Davis, *Dictionary of Wandsworth* (1900), 15.

Working Lives
1. SAC vol. 18 (1903), 117; *Calendar of Assize records; Surrey indictments: Elizabeth* (1980), No. 839; NRO, SOX 301, 1653 Kitchin to Cripps; WNQ 24; PRO, C 8/304/96.
2. PRO, PROB 4/6652.
3. H. Osborn, *Inn and around London* (1991), 4-7.
4. *Ibid.*; information from Helen Osborn.
5. Directories; 1838 tithe map; PRs; Edwards, 26; WH 5 (1972), 6-7; WBN 2/12/1988, 1.
6. J. Aubrey, *The natural history and antiquities of the County of Surrey* (1719), vol. 1, 14; PRs; PRO, E 179/188/489A; NRO, SOX 282, 1687 deed; NRO, SOX 20, indenture 1720; Rocque's map.

7. PRO, PROB 4/8676; PRO, PROB 11/341, q.16; C. Holmes, *The Eastern Association in the English Civil War* (1974), 151; PRO, SP 25/118, ff. 83, 95.
8. PRO, E 112/521, No. 144; R.J. Milward, *Wimbledon in the time of the Civil War* (1976), 61; A.W.C. Hallen, *An account of the family of Hallen or Holland* (1885), 55, 57, 64.
9. Huguenot Society *Proceedings*, vol. 1 (1887), 232-3.
10. H. Hamilton, *The English brass and copper industries to 1800* (1926), 148; HH 20 p. 258; PRO, C 11/1472/32; NRO, Spencer MR, Wandsworth freehold rental 1761-5; Camden Society, 2nd ser., vol. 44 (1889), 171.
11. PRO, LR 2/190, ff. 11-25.
12. PRs; PRO, C 5/164/81; PRO, PROB 5/2027.
13. LA, deed 196, with LMA, P95/ALL1/45, rate list at start; NRO, Spencer MR, Wandsworth freehold rental 1755; directories.
14. LA, deed 5758; HH 64 p.90, 71 p.236, 83 p.271, 96 p.231, 108, p.95, 117 p.315.
15. VCH vol. 2, 368-9; PRO, C 5/538/81; Lambeth Palace Library, E10/20 and G40/2/1; PRO, PROB 11/343, q. 130; NRO, SOX 277, 1687 deed.
16. C.T. Davis, *Industries of Wandsworth* (1898), 7-8.
17. WLHC, MS vol. on Wandsworth marriages.
18. LA, deed 5763; J. Malcolm, *A compendium of husbandry ... Surrey* (1805), vol. 1, 7-8; PRO, B3/122, with land taxes.
19. NRO, SOX 277, deed 1744; D. Lysons, *The environs of London* (1792), vol. 1, 503; HH; directories.
20. SRS vol. 25 (1964), 62.
21. VCH vol. 2, 377; 1851 census; 1871 census for Wimbledon.
22. VCH vol. 2, 363; Lysons, *Environs*, vol. 1, 503.
23. WNQ 145; Sun 22/39754; NRO, SOX 277, deed of 1705; WLHC, MS vol. on Wandsworth marriages, 8; LA, deed 5753.
24. K.G. Farries and M.T. Mason, *The windmills of Surrey and inner London* (1966), 215-18; LMA, prints (Burns cuttings 1789); WH 61 (1990), 20-1.
25. Land taxes.
26. NRO, Spencer MR, Wandsworth freehold rental 1740; Sun 259/388081, 334/514311; O. Manning and W. Bray, *The history and antiquities of the County of Surrey*, vol. 3 (1814), 342; land taxes.
27. WNQ 209-10, 245-6; NRO, SOX 277, deed 1745; 1838 tithe map.

Surrey Iron Railway
Derek A. Bayliss, *Retracing the first public railway* (1985).
Charles E. Lee, *Early railways in Surrey* (Railway Gazette, 1944).
HLRO, 1846 Commons vol. 40, Surrey Iron Dissolving Railway Bill.

1. LA, deed 5788; WHS Collection, 1659; NRO, SOX 342, Surrey Iron Railway map; Bayliss, 44.
2. HLRO, subscription list.
3. Compare 1787 Corris map.

Villas and Mansions
Edwards, 14, 25-8.
Wandsworth tithe map 1838.
WH 60 (1990), 6-19 (West Hill).

1. PRO, E 179/188/481.
2. NRO, SOX 277, 1705 and 1732 deeds.
3. DCR; SRO Guildford, 145/Box 17, Extract Book (hereafter EB), 2, 76, 111-15; LMA, Acc 976/203.
4. LMA, Q/PSN/1-6; DCR; EB, 16, 41-2, 45, 48.
5. SRO Guildford, 145/Box 13, Blakiston auction; WNQ 127; Clement Attlee, *As it happened* (1956), 8.
6. NRO, SOX 216, abstract of title; NRO, SOX 24, plan of farm, 1797.
7. Springfield Estate papers, 1815 deed.
8. DCR; EB, 9-12; LMA, Acc 1720; SAC vol.10 (1891), 102.

9. SRO Guildford, 145/Box 13, Blakiston auction.
10. WHNS 1961/5.
11. VCH vol.4, 116; DCR 19 Nov. 1726; EB, 36-7; A. St Hill, *The history of the Sainthill family* (c.1938); PRO, PROB 3/622/502.
12. *The trial of Fanny Wilmot* (1791); Coward, 42; Loobey, 29.
13. WBN Handbooks (1911-13), No.3, 7-9.
14. WH 44 (1985), 10.
15. C.T. Davis, *Dictionary of Wandsworth* (1900), 1.
16. WNQ 212.
17. LA, deed 14823.
18. WH 21 (1979), 1-3.

Mayors of Garratt
Anthony Shaw, *The Mayor of Garratt* (1980).
WH 54 (1988), 9-19.
History Today (Feb 1983), 15-23.

From Town to Suburb
London County Council, *Names of streets and places in the administrative County of London* (4th edn. 1955).
Booth.
1891 census.
Unpublished research by Keith Bailey on Southfields Grid and on District Surveyors' returns.

1. Information from Keith Bailey.
2. LA, deed 13496.
3. Loobey, 62, 68, 72, 75, 77.
4. *Kelly's London suburban directory for 1902*.
5. WNQ 21-3.
6. Coward, 55; WH 15 (1977), 8.
7. WLHC, sale catalogues volume.
8. WLHC, 613.5 PB.
9. A. Lindsay Glegg, *Four score ... and more* (1962), 13.
10. WH 2 (1971), 2-3; Joan Budman, *Jenny Lind: a biography* (1956), 300-11.
11. WH 41 (1984), 1-6; WNQ 45-9.
12. F.E. Hardy, *The life of Thomas Hardy 1840-1928* (1962), 118-20, 145-6, 149.
13. WHNS 1966/5.
14. WHNS 1965/3.
15. W.R.P. George, *Lloyd George, backbencher* (1983), 296, 337, 447; WN vol. 1, 165; WN vol. 8, 107.
16. C. Attlee, *As it happened* (1956), 7-27; T. Burridge, *Clement Attlee: a political biography* (1985), 47.
17. G.B. Longstaff, *The Langstaffs of Teesdale and Weardale* (1923), 94-126.

On the Move
Tim Sherwood, *Change at Clapham Junction* (1994).
Charles S. Dunbar, *Tramways in Wandsworth and Battersea* (1971).
WHNS 1960/6 (trams).
WH 49 (1986), 8-13 (District Railway).

1. PRO, C 8/216/59; Edwards, 27; directories; HLRO, Commons 1845 vol.65, LSWR Metropolitan Extension, 3 June, 108; WVM 1847, pp.15, 17.
2. HLRO (as note 1), 93, 110.
3. Booth, 200.
4. WBN 21/12/1889, 6a.
5. WHNS 1970/90; HLRO, Lords 1867 vol.1, Wandsworth Bridge Bill, 18 Mar, 3-7; Coward, 35.
6. WHNS 1970/90; WN vol.12, 173, 175.
7. C.T. Davis, *Industries of Wandsworth* (1898), 39.
8. HLRO, Commons 1906 vol. 10, LCC (Tramways and Improvements) Bill, 27 Apr, 108, 111.
9. NRO, SOX 439, particulars of leases; WVM 19 Oct 1749, 17 June 1753, 12 Dec 1759, 13 Mar 1783, 20 Nov 1799.

10. HLRO, Main Papers, 14 May 1811, Southwark Bridge Bill, 29-30; D.A. Bayliss, *Retracing the first public railway* (1985), 15; WBN 31/10/1958.
11. HLRO, Lords 1866 vol.4, Wandsworth Canal Bill, 40, 49, 52.

Civic Life
Janet Roebuck, *Urban development in 19th-century London* (1979).
WLHC, annual reports and annual sanitary reports of Wandsworth District Board of Works.

1. WH 56 (1988), 15-18.
2. WBN 25/1/1985, 20.
3. PP 1852 vol.12, 743-7.
4. C.T. Davis, *Dictionary of Wandsworth* (1900), 11.
5. PP 1852 vol.12, 744.
6. British Library, Althorp Papers P2; WVM 6 Apr 1755, 10 Jan 1759, 1820 p.166; Davis, *Dictionary*, 24.
7. London Topographical Society *Newsletter* 35 (1992), 3; WLHC, enquiry file, Wandsworth police.
8. *Ibid.*; letter from Clare Graham to Wandsworth Museum; H. Osborn, *Inn and around London* (1991), 124.
9. Davis, *Dictionary*, 14; Coward, 36.
10. PP 1835 vol.43, 956; Coward, 37-9.
11. M.B. of Wandsworth, *Official guide* (1948); WLHC, libraries file.
12. Huguenot Society *Proceedings*, vol.1 (1887), 229-32; WH 53 (1987), 12; WBN Handbooks (1911-13), No.2, 3-4.
13. Coward, 43-4; WVM 1853, p.210.

Churches and Chapels
Booth.
A. Lass, *Notes on the rise and progress of Methodism in Wandsworth* (1904).

1. SAC vol.18 (1903), 135; SAC vol.19 (1906), 183, 187; LMA, P95/ALL1/44, ff.315, 372; SAC vol.20 (1907); WNQ 146-7.
2. B.F.L. Clarke, *Parish churches of London* (1966), 274.
3. W.J. Edwards, *Wandsworth meeting house* (1937), 5-9; WLHC, Quaker exhibition catalogue (1973); J. Besse, *A collection of the sufferings of the people called Quakers* (1753), vol.1, 701; SAC vol.39 (1931), 101.
4. R.A. Shaw *et al*, *Huguenots in Wandsworth* (1985), 13; Huguenot Society *Proceedings*, vol.22 (1976), 552; *ibid.*, vol.1 (1887), 240-1.
5. SRS vol.34 (1994), 145; C.T. Davis, *The Memorial Hall, Wandsworth* (1913), 9-11, 14; plaque on Memorial Hall.
6. WNQ 131.
7. Loobey, 10.
8. LMA, rpp/DW/D(3); Coward, 12-14.
9. WVM 16 Sept 1819; I. Caudwell, *The pepper-pot church: St Anne's, Wandsworth* (1946), 4-12.
10. LMA, P95/MRY2/48; *The parish of St Mary Summerstown ...* (1954).
11. R. Milward, *'This most extraordinary mission'* (1991).
12. PRO, HO 129/32.
13. Clarke, *Parish churches*, 274-8.
14. *Wandsworth Parish Magazine*, June 1963.
15. Coward, 11, 14-15; WBN 13/2/1970.
16. R. Mudie-Smith (ed), *The religious life of London* (1904).
17. *Ibid.*; PP 1901 vol.51, 829; A.L. Glegg, *Four score ... and more* (1962), 13.
18. *Ibid.*, 16-21.
19. WLHC, notes.

Educating Wandsworth
W.I. Moore, *The story of All Saints' Schools, Wandsworth* (1909).
WBN Handbooks (1911-13), No.4, 17-20.
LMA, records of London School Board and LCC.
WLHC, card index.

1. LMA, P95/ALL1/44, 258, 271; PRO, STAC 8/298/25 with LMA, E/BER/S/TII/B1/10.
2. PRO, PROB 11/547, q.150.
3. PP 1819 vol.9 part 2.
4. Wyld's map of London's environs 1849; PP 1901 vol.51, 820.
5. C.T. Davis, *History of the British School, Wandsworth* (1900).
6. W.J. Edwards, *Wandsworth meeting house* (1937), 16; SAC vol.39 (1931), 101; Edwards, 26.
7. Edwards, 25-8; D. Lysons, *The environs of London* (1792), vol.1, 511.
8. PP 1819 vol.9 part 2; PRO, ED 3/16.
9. WLHC, misc. file W378.99 WAN; Davis, *British School*, 14.
10. G.B. Longstaff, *The Langstaffs of Teesdale and Weardale* (1923), 116; directories.
11. WLHC, programme for opening of extension to Wandsworth Technical Institute 1936; PP 1901 vol.51, 824; WLHC, card index.
12. M. Williams, *The Society of the Sacred Heart* (1978), 118, 132, 167; Loobey, 29, 119.

The Poor and the Sick

Coward.
WH 9 (1973) (RVPA).

1. SAC vol.17 (1902), 162, 165; SAC vol.20 (1907), 204; SAC vol.39 (1931), 101-2.
2. VCH vol.2, 110; LMA, P95/ALL1/45.
3. PP 1901 vol.51, 803-4, 826.
4. WVM 1730-1, 13 July 1748.
5. Sir Richard Phillips, *A morning's walk from London to Kew* (1820), 107-9.
6. Westminster Archives, G1002, 539, 541, 553; *ibid.*, G1003, 245, 247, 250, 295.
7. WLHC, enquiry file, St John's Hospital; WBN 26/12/1885.
8. WLHC, misc. file 725.55 WAN.
9. I.L. Patch, *Springfield: a short history* (1985); 1851 census.
10. *Notes and sketches: a century in the life of the Royal Hospital ...* (1981).
11. WLHC, cuttings etc. on the RVPA.

Wandsworth Prison

H. Mayhew and J. Binny, *The criminal prisons of London* (1862).
Coward, 26-34.
Unpublished research by Stewart McLaughlin.

1. WLHC, cuttings etc.; information from Wandsworth Prison.

Open Spaces

Shirley Passmore, *Wandsworth Common* (typescript, 1995).
How the Battle of Wandsworth Common was fought and won (c.1887).

1. NRO, SOX 101, 1758 lease; WVM, 6 & 10 Mar 1782; LA, deed 14823.
2. e.g. NRO, SOX 101, 1760 lease to Joseph Wight.
3. WVM, 24 Nov 1802; NRO, SOX 330 (3), plan and survey 1802.
4. WLHC, A.712 CLA.
5. NRO, SOX 216.
6. WN vol. 12, 13.
7. WN vol. 12, 13-16.
8. NRO, SOX 216; LCC, *London parks and open spaces* (1906), 14, 21.
9. WLHC, brochure for opening of park.
10 WN vol. 2, 6; WLHC, enquiry file, Earlsfield.
11. Information from R.J. Milward.
12. WN vol. 8, 31-2; WLHC, card index.

Wandsworth at Play

'Wandsworth pubs', WH (forthcoming).

1. Edwards, 26.
2. H. Osborn, *Inn and around London* (1991), 123-4; *The Times*, 17/12/1828, 3d; WVM 1847, p.17; Coward, 14; WBN, 18/10/1890, 5d.
3. WLHC, Petty Sessions minutes.
4. WN vol. 2, 1; WLHC, misc. file 725.74; M.B. of Wandsworth, *Official guide* (1960).
5. Osborn, *Inn*, 124; Booth, 219; notes by Elaine Horwood of English Heritage; WBN 7 & 14/10/60; WLHC, misc. file, cinemas.
6. WLHC, misc. file 791.42; M. Webb, *The Amber Valley gazetteer of Greater London's suburban cinemas 1946-86* (1986); WLHC, card index; Loobey, 12.
7. WLHC, enquiry file.
8. SAC vol. 19 (1906), 157; LMA, P95/ALL1/45, 1658/9; J. Goulstone, *Early club and village cricket* (1972); NRO, SOX 216.
9. WLHC, card index; WNQ 105; WHS Collection, 1478; Wandsworth Museum exhibition 1998; Loobey, 95.
10. P. Loobey, *Flights of fancy: early aviation in Battersea and Wandsworth* (1981), 8-10.

New Industries for Old

C.T. Davis, *Industries of Wandsworth* (1898).
The Wandsworth and District Gas Company: a centenary of progress 1834-1934 (1934).
Directories.

1. WN vol.9, 190; HLRO, 1866 Lords vol. 12, Wandsworth & Putney Gas Bill, 11 June, p.6.
2. *Ibid.*, pp. 174-85.
3. WBN 2/2/1940, 3; WN vol. 8, 103.
4   LMA, Acc 1037/730/4-6.
5. Jo Stanley and Bronwen Griffiths, *For love and shillings: Wandsworth women's working lives* (1990), 143-9.
6. PP 1888 vol. 87.
7. Stanford's map of London 1891; OS map 1894.
8. WLHC, misc. file 388.4.
9. P. Loobey, *Flights of fancy: early aviation in Battersea and Wandsworth* (1981), 23-6.
10. G.A. Dummett, *From little acorns: a history of the A.P.V. Company Limited* (1981).
11. WH 55 (1988), 8-15.
12. Dummett, *From little acorns*, 140; WBN 2/12/1988.

Modern Wandsworth

M.B. of Wandsworth, *Official guide* (1948, 1953 and 1959 editions).
London County Council, *Names of streets and places in the administrative County of London* (4th edn. 1955).

1. Electoral registers.
2. 1991 census.
3. WBN 3/6/1938, 6, 28/8/1964, 1, 19/3/1993, 11.
4. WBN 15/8/1969, 1, 3/10/1969,8.
5. *Wandsworth Society Newsletter*, May/June 1978.
6. *Ibid.*, Jan 1972, March 1997.